IMAGES
of America

ART DECO OF THE PALM BEACHES

The Jazzman is an original limited-edition serigraph (silk screen) of 200 signed and numbered images by the artist Sharon Koskoff. The 32-inch-high by 40-inch-wide tap dancing symbol was transformed into the logo for the Art Deco Society of the Palm Beaches. *The Jazzman* has been seen on book covers, programs, murals, T-shirts, and needlepoint. The oversized serigraph was printed in 1987 and appeared on the cover of *Sunshine Artists Magazine* in April 1988. Koskoff coined the word "Decometric" in 1980, to describe original art and design made in the late 20th century that imitates the Art Deco style.

ON THE COVER: Sun worshippers recline at the tropical Beach Terrace Apartments on South Ocean Boulevard in Delray Beach. Throughout history, the sun was worshipped as a god whose benevolence provided warmth and made the crops grow. Historically, the upper classes went to great lengths to limit their exposure to the sun. In 1920s France, the caramel-skinned entertainer Josephine Baker became a Parisian idol. Concurrently, fashion designer Coco Chanel was "bronzed" while cruising on a yacht. A winter tan became a symbol of the leisure class and showed you could afford to travel to exotic climates. South Florida cities "boomed" in the Art Deco era, as Northerners vacationed in the sun-filled Palm Beaches. (Courtesy of the Delray Beach Historical Society.)

IMAGES
of America

ART DECO OF THE PALM BEACHES

Sharon Koskoff

ARCADIA
PUBLISHING

Published by Arcadia Publishing
Charleston, South Carolina

Library of Congress Catalog Card Number: 2006938293

For all general information contact Arcadia Publishing at:
Telephone 843-853-2070
Fax 843-853-0044
E-mail sales@arcadiapublishing.com
For customer service and orders:
Toll-Free 1-888-313-2665

Visit us on the Internet at www.arcadiapublishing.com

This book is dedicated to Barbara Baer Capitman, whose guidance encouraged me to develop the Art Deco Society of the Palm Beaches. I also want to dedicate this book to my parents, Shirley and Rubin "Poppa Ruby" Koskoff, who are always there to support my endeavors.

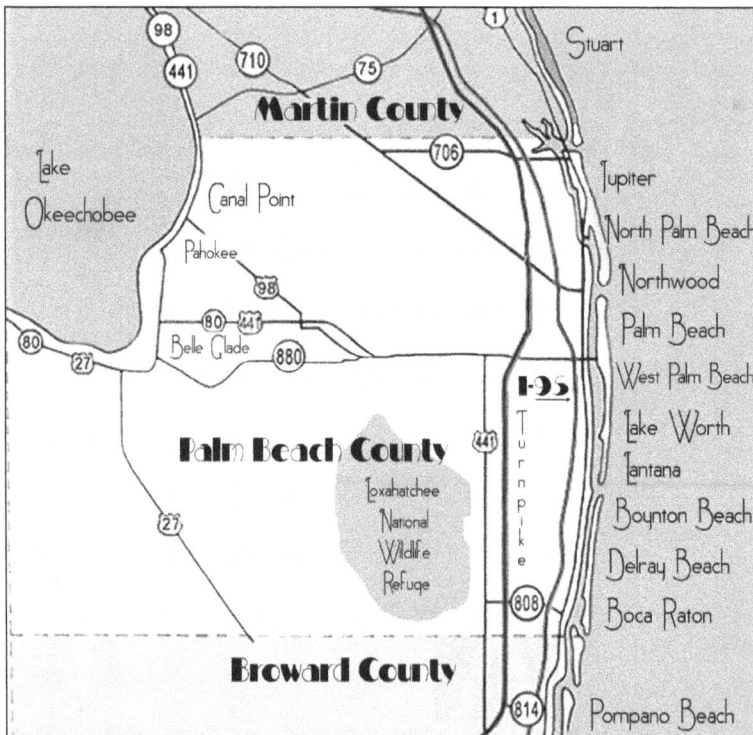

The Palm Beach County map in this book highlights the cities where Art Deco architecture is discovered. Modernism is found on the eastern seaboard, the western lakefront, and to the north in Martin County.

CONTENTS

ACKNOWLEDGMENTS

Art Deco of the Palm Beaches contains 204 photographs that were chosen for their historical significance. This book was written to educate and visually entertain while fulfilling the need to compile a comprehensive record of Modernism in the Palm Beaches.

Special thanks goes to Linda Fleetwood, my friend and mentor, who spent days editing to help make this book a reality. I could not have gotten through the crazy days, nights, and catastrophes without her supportive efforts.

I am grateful for the assistance from my three editors at Arcadia Publishing: Adam Ferrell, Ingrid Powell, and Lauren Bobier. (As you know, everything in Art Deco happens in groups of three.)

An appreciation award goes to all of the great people below, who trusted me with their precious photographs, who allowed me to borrow and scan them, who returned my multiple phone calls and e-mails, who drove me around the county, who opened their homes to further preservation efforts, and who gave me advice on "how to" write the book:

Amy Clyman	Janet De Vries
Ann O'Connell Rust	Jean and Sumner Draper
Anne Weir	Jillian Papa
Beverly Mustaine	Joyce Goldman
Carolyn S. Denton	Kirby Kooluris
Cheryl and Homer Marshman	LaVaine Wrigley
Christian Davenport	Linda Fleetwood
David Edgar	Linda Stabile
Diane Freaney	Loretta Smith
Dorothy Patterson	Mark Smith
Dr. Joseph Orsenigo	Rhonda and Tek Shoumate

All photographs are taken from the archives of the Art Deco Society of the Palm Beaches and are photographed by Sharon Koskoff, unless otherwise noted.

ABOUT THE AUTHOR

Sharon Koskoff is a freelance writer and lecturer on the stylings of Twentieth Century design. She is a professional visual artist known for her public murals, conceptual installations, children's programming, and preservation efforts. Koskoff is the chairperson of the Public Art Advisory Board in Delray Beach, Florida. She graduated from Brooklyn College (1974) and the New York School of Interior Design (1977). The immense variety of Sharon's artwork can be seen in depth on her Web site www.BySharon.com.

INTRODUCTION

Art Deco of the Palm Beaches is about Modernism and the beginnings of Twentieth Century design. Art is a reflection of society, and in the 1920s, 1930s, and 1940s, the world put aside conventional values and supported new ideologies. Traditional forms of art, architecture, and social organization were swept away. Art Deco was a revolt against the feminine, flowery, and curvaceous Art Nouveau movement. In the 1890s, soft, fluid forms found in nature were typified with voluptuous women draped in long flowing hair entwined with vines of ivy. The emancipating Jazz Age now featured images of thin women with "boyish" bodies and "bobbed" haircuts, drinking martinis and posing with elongated cigarette holders.

The mechanized age of Modernism gave way to new aesthetics and an improved way of making things. Prior to the Industrial Revolution, all objects were made by hand. Mass production efforts tried to recreate one-of-a-kind items but failed. However, the machine could do something the hand could not do—make a straight line. Art Deco unfolded as a masculine, hard-edge, geometrical "linear" celebration. Designers looked back into all of art history and studied the forms of Aztec, Mayan, Japanese, and other geometrically styled cultures. Howard Carter discovered King Tutankhamen's tomb in 1922, which contributed to the popularity of Egyptian motifs, pyramids, and using groups of three in design.

In the early 20th century, jewelry, ceramics, fashion, furniture, lighting, and everything from automobiles to radios were under the influence of the new wave called Modernism. Visual artists from Picasso to Mondrian experimented with straight lines, angles, and the geometry of Cubism. Travel was popular, and African safaris brought jungle skins into the home. Fast animals associated with speed such as the gazelle, jaguar, and whippet were reflected in design. Stylized images of airplanes, automobiles, cruise liners, and skyscrapers emerged. The French ocean liner the *Normandie* was launched in 1932 as the largest and fastest ship in the world. The glamorous silver screen days of Hollywood dazzled audiences with stars like Fred Astaire, Ginger Rogers, Marlene Dietrich, and Greta Garbo.

The term Art Deco was first coined in November 1966 by Hilary Gelson in the *Times* (London) as the United States was experiencing a reemergence of the streamlined style. It was made popular by Bevis Hillier in 1968, when he wrote *Art Deco of the 20s and 30s*, published by Studio Vista. Art Deco was taken from the *Exposition Internationale des Arts Decoratifs et Industriels Modernes* held in Paris in 1925. Art Deco became a catch-all phrase for everything that was designed or built from 1925 until 1939. The outbreak of World War II required the halt of frivolity, and all manufacturing was concentrated on the war machine.

Architecturally there is a myriad of styles categorized under the umbrella of Art Deco. All of these styles have their own unique qualities, although the names are often interchanged. These include Art Moderne, German Bauhaus, Depression Moderne, International Style, Jazz Age, Machine Age, Moderne, Moorish Deco, Nautical Deco, Neoclassical, Pueblo Deco, Roaring Twenties, Streamline Moderne, Tropical Deco, Zig-Zag, and more.

The majority of modern architecture found in South Florida is actually Streamline Moderne. Art Deco has a vertical orientation with emphasis on applied decoration, while Streamline Moderne concentrates on the horizontal and the absence of man's "idiosyncratic" embellishments. A fascination with speed combined with South Florida's water-based environment left an aerodynamic and nautical imprint on the architecture. "Eyebrows," flat linear planes that look like shelves placed over windows, are elements indigenous of South Florida architecture. Rounded corners, racing stripes, flat roofs, bandings, eyebrows, portholes, and stepped pediments are also emphasized throughout Palm Beach County.

Europe is rich with history, and its buildings have lasted for several centuries. However, in South Florida, the oldest existing structures are less than 100 years old. The exceptional styles of Modernism have been discovered all through the county. If these treasures are to be forgotten, a wealth of history and a vital connection to the past will be lost forever. Therefore, it is essential that the Art Deco heritage of Palm Beach County be protected, preserved, and allowed to continue to flourish into the future.

On January 16, 1992, the Art Deco Society of the Palm Beaches held a gala fund-raiser at the historic Lake Worth Playhouse. Members fashioned in Roaring Twenties attire are, from left to right, Loretta Smith (special events), Mark Smith (vice president), Sharon Koskoff (president), Tony Crosby, and Amy Clyman (secretary). The Dazzling Decadent Dessert Bar followed a special benefit performance of *Painting Churches*, coordinated by Jan Engelhardt (playhouse manager).

One

ART DECO
"ARTS" BUILDINGS
(COUNTYWIDE)

Palm Beach County has hundreds of Art Deco buildings located in the older downtown sections of its cities. The largest and most treasured jewels house important not-for-profit visual and performing arts institutions. The county's Art Deco heritage lives on through these significant arts organizations and their respected patrons.

The Boyd Building, the Norton Gallery and School of Art (Norton Museum of Art), the Oakley Theatre (Lake Worth Playhouse), Palm Beach High School (Alexander W. Dreyfoos Jr. High School of the Arts), and the Prince Theatre were built as arts organizations and continue operating within their intended arts purpose. Other arts facilities are what preservationists call an "adaptive reuse," where a historic building is renovated and restored for a new purpose. These include the Florida Theatre (Cuillo Centre for the Performing Arts), the Old West Palm Beach National Guard Armory (Armory Art Center), the Lake Avenue Theatre (Palm Beach Institute of Contemporary Art), and the Martin County Courthouse (Martin County Council of the Arts).

Many venues may have changed their name, color, signage, or mission, while others have expanded campuses with new additions. However, all of the structures maintain their historical integrity and continue to keep the "Art" in Art Deco.

Art Deco design strips away classical elements of architecture, leaving lettering and relief as ornamentation. Mythological characters are frequently seen in modern design to symbolize and enhance a structure's identity. Paul Manship's *Imagination* (above) and *Interpretation* (below) are words of wisdom inscribed on these personified Art Deco bas-reliefs at the Norton Museum of Art. The horizontal reliefs enhance the niches on the east facade of the gallery, framing the nickel-bronze sculptures of *Diana* and *Actaeon* (shown on pages 12 and 13 respectively). Originally the Manship sculptures had aesthetically placed *Actaeon* on the left and *Diana* on the right. In early spring 2002, the pair was reversed to their historically correct position with *Diana* on the left pointing her bow at *Actaeon*. The Norton Museum of Art is located in West Palm Beach at 1451 South Olive Avenue. (Courtesy of Norton Museum of Art.)

C-35—Norton Gallery of Art, West Palm Beach, Fla.

In 1940, Ralph Hubbard Norton (1875–1953) and his wife, Elizabeth Calhoun Norton (1881–1947), commissioned Marion Syms Wyeth of the distinguished firm of Wyeth and King to design a building to house their art collection in West Palm Beach. The Norton Gallery and School of Art opened to the public on February 8, 1941. The name was changed to the Norton Museum of Art in the 1990s. The permanent collection of over 5,000 works consists of European, American, and Chinese art and artifacts, Modern and contemporary art, and photography. In January 1997, the museum completed an expansion and renovation that more than doubled the size of the existing museum, selecting Centerbrook Architects and Planners to design the project. In March 2003, Chad Floyd, of Centerbrook Architects, designed the Gail and Melvin Nessel Wing, which houses a permanent glass ceiling installation commissioned from Dale Chihuly. (Courtesy of Norton Museum of Art.)

Paul Manship (1885–1966) is known for embracing the true Art Deco style, depicting speed and streamlining in the name of progress and modernity. In 1925, he created these nickel-bronze masterpieces of *Diana* and *Actaeon*. The Norton casts of *Diana* and *Actaeon* were purchased in 1940 through the Palm Beach Art League Construction Account. The rare and complete pair of sculptures is the largest scale of several versions created. According to Greco-Roman mythology, Actaeon was a mortal hunter who one day came upon Diana (identified with the Greek goddess Artemis), the Roman goddess of hunting, animals, and virgins, while she was bathing nude. Enraged by this invasion of privacy, the goddess shot him with an arrow that transformed him into a stag. Unable to recognize his identity, Actaeon's own hounds then tore him to pieces. In Manship's version of *Actaeon*, he is still mostly human in form, with only the shapes of his ears and a pair of budding antlers indicating that the change to stag has begun. (Courtesy of Preservation Foundation of Palm Beach/Norton Museum of Art.)

Paul Manship was born in St. Paul, Minnesota, and studied painting at the St. Paul Institute of Art from 1892 to 1903, when color blindness shifted his focus to sculpture. In 1905, he studied anatomy in New York City and won the prestigious Prix de Rome at the age of 24. This prize sent him to the American Academy in Rome for three years. His distinctive classical style was inspired by mythology and the archaic sculpture of Greece and Rome. Manship returned to New York in 1912 where he became a major success. Paul Manship's most familiar icon is the exultant *Prometheus* fountain, completed in 1934, at the heart of New York's Rockefeller Center. Others include the memorial gates for the New York Bronx Zoological Park, the *Time and the Fates* sundial of the 1939 World's Fair, and the charming Aesop's fables adorning the Osborne Memorial Playground Gateway in New York's Central Park. Manship continued to receive commissions up until the time of his death. (Courtesy of Preservation Foundation of Palm Beach/Norton Museum of Art.)

In West Palm Beach, architect William Manly King built the Vocational Arts Building on 300 Gardenia Street as Palm Beach High School in 1941. This is the only Art Deco–styled building on the campus of 10 other historic structures now known as the Alexander W. Dreyfoos Jr. School of the Arts. The above photograph profiles the grand entrance displaying a stepped roofline, columns, and sets of three. The facade below displays four small bas-reliefs that symbolize, from left to right, film production, communications, drafting, and printing. In 1988, the school board wanted to demolish the building. The Art Deco Society of the Palm Beaches fought for two years to preserve the institution for future generations. The building currently houses the School of the Arts Foundation, the Visual Arts Department, and a small art gallery.

Central Schools (1908), became Palm Beach High School in 1915 and then Twin Lakes High School in the 1960s. The Sapodilla Avenue arch, built in 1922 by William Manly King, personifies both visual and performing arts. A male figure (left) holds brushes while painting, and a female figure sports a violin and bow. Since 1997, Dreyfoos School of the Arts is an arts magnet that draws students from throughout the county.

The cornerstone marker on the vocational building states that William Manly King was the architect of the building, erected in 1941. Centered is the Masonry or Freemasonry logo that symbolizes justice, equality, and compassion for humanity. King was a well-known architect of institutional buildings in Palm Beach County, having also designed the Old West Palm Beach National Guard Armory and Canal Point Elementary School.

15

The formal opening of the Prince Theatre was May 28, 1931, in Pahokee, along the Okeechobee River in western Palm Beach County. Local architect Chester Cone designed the building at 227 East Main Street. The first movie shown was *The Return of Frank James*, and admission was only 35¢. Up until recently, the now vacant building, owned by the town, was being used for community activities.

The Lake Theatre at 601 Lake Avenue in Lake Worth opened in 1939, and it was built by architect Roy A. Benjamin (1888–1963). He was born in Ocala and moved to Jacksonville in 1902. He is credited with designing other theaters in the Southeast. The movie house was operated by E. J. Sparks, a subsidiary of Paramount Pictures. During the 1960s, the theater turned into an eatery called the Pasta Palace.

J. Patrick Lannan renovated the Art Deco movie theater in 1980 to house his collection of contemporary art and design. After his death in 1983, the Lannan Foundation, chaired by his son, J. Patrick Lannan Jr., resumed the museum's mission. In 1989, the foundation and a majority of the collection were relocated to Los Angeles. The building and a collection of American craft objects, kinetic art from the 1960s and 1970s, and a commissioned Tom Otterness frieze, *Battle of the Sexes*, were then donated to Palm Beach Community College. In July 1999, philanthropists Robert M. and Mary Montgomery purchased, renovated, and heroically created the Palm Beach Institute of Contemporary Art. It became the premier locale for contemporary arts and a link to the New York art world before its closure on March 27, 2005.

In 1985, Don McKin (on the roof) and Jim Ferguson (on the ladder) work at permanently removing the upper portion of the Lake Worth Playhouse sign. The lower lettering is made of neon, a significant invention of the Machine Age developed in Paris by engineer Georges Claude (1870–1960). In 1923, his French company, Claude Neon, introduced neon gas signs to the United States. (Courtesy of the Lake Worth Playhouse.)

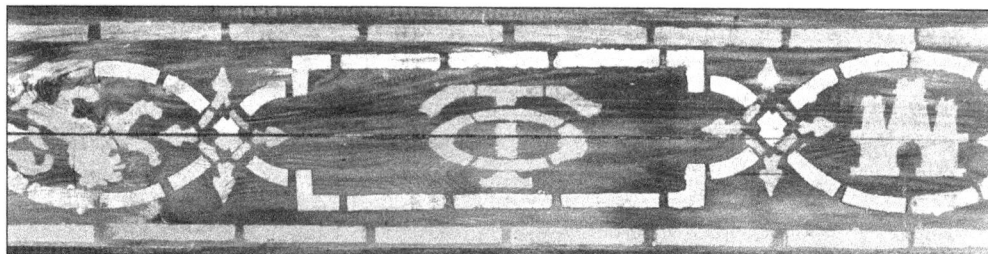

Formerly the Oakley Theatre, the Lake Worth Playhouse at 713 Lake Avenue still has its distinctive pecky cypress beams supporting the ceiling. Pecky cypress is an innovation of the early 20th century and is found in many Southern historic structures. The initials "O" and "T" stenciled in an overlapping design stand for the Oakley Theatre. (Courtesy of the Lake Worth Playhouse.)

The Oakley Theatre, built in 1924, stands in the Moorish Deco style before damaged by the hurricane on September 16, 1928. The building was constructed by brothers Clarence and Lucian Oakley from Illinois. The Depression struck in 1929, just as the theater reopened. Clarence committed suicide in 1931 because of financial troubles. Ironically, Lucian died one year later to the day. It is believed that their ghosts still wander the playhouse halls.

In October 1975, the Lake Worth Playhouse purchased the Oakley Theatre building for $60,000. In this photograph, the theater gets a fresh coat of paint and a new color scheme. *The Last of Mrs. Lincoln* was the first play produced in the new venue. The all-volunteer community theater group was first established in 1953 and performed in the Municipal Auditorium of city hall. (Courtesy of the Lake Worth Playhouse.)

The Lake Worth Playhouse, as it is shown in this 1980s photograph, was rebuilt and modified to a sleek Streamline design in 1929. The horizontal bandings and vertical columns create symmetry and a modern statement. In 2007, the playhouse will undergo another transformation, and it will add a new neon marquee in the historic Art Deco style. (Courtesy of the Lake Worth Playhouse.)

The Cuillo Centre for the Arts, 201 Clematis Street, West Palm Beach, was originally the Florida Theatre, showing motion pictures from 1949 to 1981. Zeidler Partnership, architects known for designing the Kravis Center for the Performing Arts, did an Art Deco renovation in the late 1990s. The Florida Theatre is often confused with the Kettler Theatre–turned Palm Theatre, across the street, which was built in 1924 and razed in 1965.

During the World War II era in West Palm Beach, the Home Guard soldiers stand before the Old West Palm Beach National Guard Armory, built in 1939 by William Manly King. The building was constructed with Works Progress Administration (WPA) funds. In the 1950s, the armory was used as a farmers market by day and entertained with dances at night. (Courtesy of the Armory Art Center/Historical Society of Palm Beach County.)

In 1987, the armory was destined for the wrecking ball. An area art school was in need of a home, so local activists saved the building. The Art Deco Society of the Palm Beaches identified the vacant structure as a rare Streamline Moderne institution. After undergoing restoration, the Armory Art Center now offers visual art workshops, gallery space, and a world-class sculpture studio at 1703 South Lake Avenue.

The Boyd Building, 824 East Atlantic Avenue, sits on Delray Beach's Intracoastal Waterway. Architect Gustav Maass built this "ocean liner" building in 1939. Originally the Boyd was the home of artists' and writers' studios. The lower level currently houses Busch's Restaurant (formerly the Bridge Restaurant, then Canal Street Grille). In 1990, owner Burton Handelsman commissioned Sharon Koskoff to create a color scheme to enhance the architectural details. See page 31.

In 1936, L. Phillip Clarke designed the Martin County Courthouse with funds from the Works Progress Administration. Symbols and inscriptions of the idealistic Roosevelt era are present in cast friezes and cornices. In 1989, the building was saved from the wrecking ball. The Martin County Council for the Arts was created featuring a gallery that rotates fine arts exhibits. The new courthouse sits directly behind the historic structure located at 80 East Ocean Boulevard, Stuart.

Two

DECO IN DELRAY BEACH (SOUTH COUNTY)

In the 1920s, the Florida land boom brought prosperity to Delray Beach. Real estate speculation and tourism were principal parts of the local economy. Delray Beach was the largest town on the east coast of Florida between West Palm Beach and Fort Lauderdale. Pineapple was the primary crop grown and is reflected in the present-day Pineapple Grove Historic Arts District on Northeast Second Avenue.

Delray Beach has undergone a renaissance of art and culture in the 1990s, with the creation of Art and Jazz on the Avenue street festivals. A large-scale renovation of shops and restaurants brought nightlife to downtown Atlantic Avenue.

The Delray Beach Historical Society preserves the city's archives and historic sites and operates the Cason Cottage Museum on Northeast First Street at Swinton Avenue. In February 1994, the society initiated the highly successful annual Antiques Show and Sale.

The Art Deco Society of the Palm Beaches conducts an art and architectural walking tour entitled Deco in Delray. Explorers start at the beach and then walk across the Intracoastal Waterway to the historic Boyd Building. The tour continues west and ends at Old School Square Cultural Arts Center at Swinton Avenue. The complex is home to the Crest Theatre, a restored 1925 gymnasium, the Cornell Museum of Art and History, and an outdoor entertainment pavilion. The buildings were designed in the Mediterranean Revival style by Sam Ogren Sr.

Delray Beach is the home base for the Art Deco Society of the Palm Beaches. Hurricane Wilma struck on Monday, October 24, 2005, causing widespread damage to homes and businesses, including the society's historical archives.

The Veterans Park Bandshell was built in the 1920s opposite the Boyd Building. The semicircular archway is banded with three stripes and a geometrical cornice. It was located on the northwest corner of the Intracoastal Waterway in downtown Delray Beach. Veterans Park currently features a community playground, gazebo, and boat docks, although the bandshell is no longer there. (Courtesy of the Delray Beach Historical Society.)

Originally built in 1923 in the Mediterranean style, the Delray Theatre movie marquee is a 1940s Art Deco addition. Straight lines, rounded corners, and sets of three, under the lettering, demonstrate this theatrical design. Located on Northeast Fifth Avenue, off East Atlantic Avenue, it was torn down in 1961. (Courtesy of the Delray Beach Historical Society.)

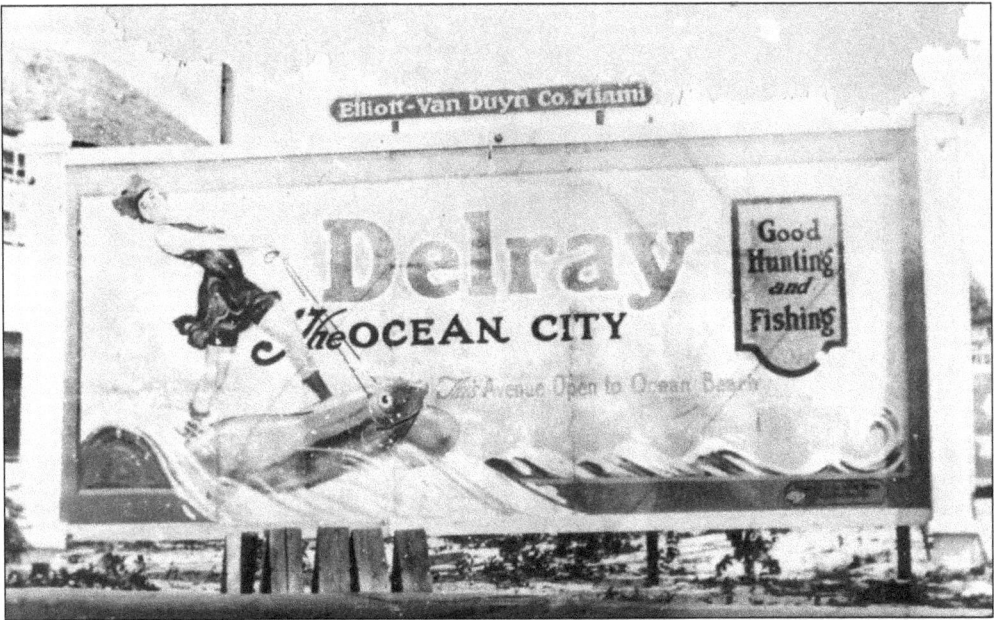

In the 1920s, the Ocean City billboard was a landmark on East Atlantic Avenue. Nicknames of Delray included "Ocean City," "Polo Capital of the World," "Gladiola Capital," and currently "Village by the Sea." The water-skiing woman is fashioned in a dashing bathing suit from the era of the suffrage movement, which prompted the right of women (over age 30) to vote. (Courtesy of the Delray Beach Historical Society.)

America's most famous streamer was the *Silver Meteor* by the Edward G. Budd Manufacturing Company, built in 1939 for the Seaboard Air Line Railroad. The deluxe passenger train featured stainless-steel coaches, modern sleeping cars, and even an onboard nurse. The train traveled from Miami to New York in 25 hours. (Courtesy of the Boynton Beach City Library.)

The Nautical Aire apartments still stand on the east side of the Intracoastal Waterway. Located at 917 Bucida Road and Seagate Drive, it catered to weekly rentals all year-round. The name of the building refers to such nautical elements as the portholes on the left side (the port side) and the streamlined facade. The flat roof and eyebrows add to its modernity. (Courtesy of the Delray Beach Historical Society.)

The tropical Beach Terrace Apartments were located at 4513 South Ocean Boulevard, also known as Highway A1A. The furnished apartments and hotel rooms boasted individually controlled air-conditioning and electric heat. The Beach Terrace Apartments are also shown on the opposite page and the book's front cover. The property is now the site of the Boca Cove Villas Condominium, built in 1981. (Courtesy of the Delray Beach Historical Society.)

Casa Las Olas was built across from the beach, at 14 South Ocean Boulevard, off East Atlantic Avenue. It was a hotel with a coffee shop and dining room built in 1937. It was only open during the seasonal winter months to accommodate Northerners seeking sunshine. The building has been altered and is now Boston's on the Beach restaurant, catering to a year-round market. (Courtesy of the Delray Beach Historical Society.)

The Beach Terrace Apartments display the brilliant use of the stepped-back motif. It is also known as Zig-Zag, pyramidal, or "lightning bolt" and is a significant Art Deco characteristic. Linear-plane eyebrows follow the staggering pattern profile. The word Zig-Zag comes from the Mesopotamian ziggurats that translates as "to build on a raised area." (Courtesy of the Delray Beach Historical Society.)

Hidden among contemporary Spanish influenced palaces, at 2225 South Ocean Boulevard, the Delray Villas are 16 detached two-bedroom apartments on the oceanfront in Delray Beach. The quaintly unique villas have a Zig-Zag facade with the same motif repeated on the side of the cottages. Built in the early 1940s, the villas featured modern amenities such as tile baths, complete

electric kitchens, and private bathing on the beach. In general, Art Deco buildings were painted solid white with a touch of blue or green trim to reflect the colors of the ocean. The clean, pure white was used to attract Northern tourists from the frosty cold winters and gloom of the Great Depression. (Courtesy of the Delray Beach Historical Society.)

Zuckerman's, established in 1926, in the Rawl and Fisher Building was Delray's first hometown department store. "Style without extravagance" was their motto. The facade's geometrical motifs were covered up in the 1950s. Currently the Mercer Wenzel Shop continues in the department store's tradition and is located at 401 East Atlantic Avenue. (Courtesy of the Delray Beach Historical Society.)

The Flamingo Service Station was built in 1939 on the railroad crossing of East Atlantic Avenue and Northeast Third Avenue. Adaptive use of a historic building converted the gas station into Elwood's Dixie Barbecue, maintaining an automotive theme with the original gas pump and grease racks. Known for its open-air ambiance and live entertainment, the restaurant has motorcyclists lining their steel-and-chrome machines outside each night. (Courtesy of the Delray Beach Historical Society.)

The Boyd Building was built in 1939 and named after Frederic E. Boyd. This photograph from the 1940s dramatizes the road and bridge expansion as the widening of East Atlantic Avenue becomes a necessity. During construction, the palm trees had to be removed in order to accommodate the progress of the "Ocean City." (Courtesy of the Delray Beach Historical Society.)

The Presidential Building, constructed in 1925, suffered some damage in the 1947 hurricane but proudly prevails today. Formerly Virginia Courtney Interiors, and currently Gringle, Doherty and Wheat, the building is located at 701 East Atlantic Avenue. Characteristics include fluted ribbed columns, bandings, and an open second-floor patio that rests above the front-door eyebrow. (Courtesy of the Delray Beach Historical Society.)

The Woman's Club of Delray Beach was founded in 1902 and moved into its new quarters at 505 South Fifth Avenue in June 1949. Several years ago, the city agreed to manage the historic structure. After renovations, Teen Central 505 was completed with an inline skating ramp and park for community youth. In 2005, the Delray Beach Youth Council with artist Sharon Koskoff painted an interior mural. (Courtesy of the Delray Beach Historical Society.)

Kwik Chek Supermarket was a predecessor to the Winn-Dixie chain. The understated structure reflects the simplicity of the town's early days and has since been demolished. The grocery was located at 114 Northeast Second Avenue, now called the Pineapple Grove Historic Arts District. Although many Moderne buildings remain in the Grove, they are in immediate danger of destruction. (Courtesy of the Delray Beach Historical Society.)

J. L. Webb built the modern Bowling Arcade in the 1930s, which also housed C. W. Hill Electric Company. Men in uniform accepted the hospitalities of the establishment throughout the duration of World War II. The arcade was built on the train tracks across from the Flamingo Service Station and was destroyed by fire in 1955. (Courtesy of the Delray Beach Historical Society.)

The third U.S. Post Office in Delray Beach was located at Northeast First Avenue across from Old School Square. In the 1980s, it was a Goodwill Store selling secondhand collectibles, and in 2001, it became Toussaint L'Ouverture High School for Arts and Social Justice. On May 30, 2006, the structure was demolished to create a city parking lot and public park. (Courtesy of the Delray Beach Historical Society.)

Mussle's Drive-In was named for Emil J. Mussle, whose family lived next door at 605 Northeast Second Street, off Federal Highway. They were known for chicken and shrimp in the basket and curb service at the barbecue restaurant drive-in. Mussle's was in operation during the 1940s and 1950s. (Courtesy of the Delray Beach Historical Society.)

The commercial Smith Brothers' Film Drop at 202 Northeast Sixth Avenue was built in 1936. The angled corner entrance is a popular feature recurring in Art Deco architecture. The left side mirrors the right side, and the center has a protruding futuristic ornamentation. The racing stripes resemble a cigar band. The original building was recently remodeled, and matching wings were added to each side.

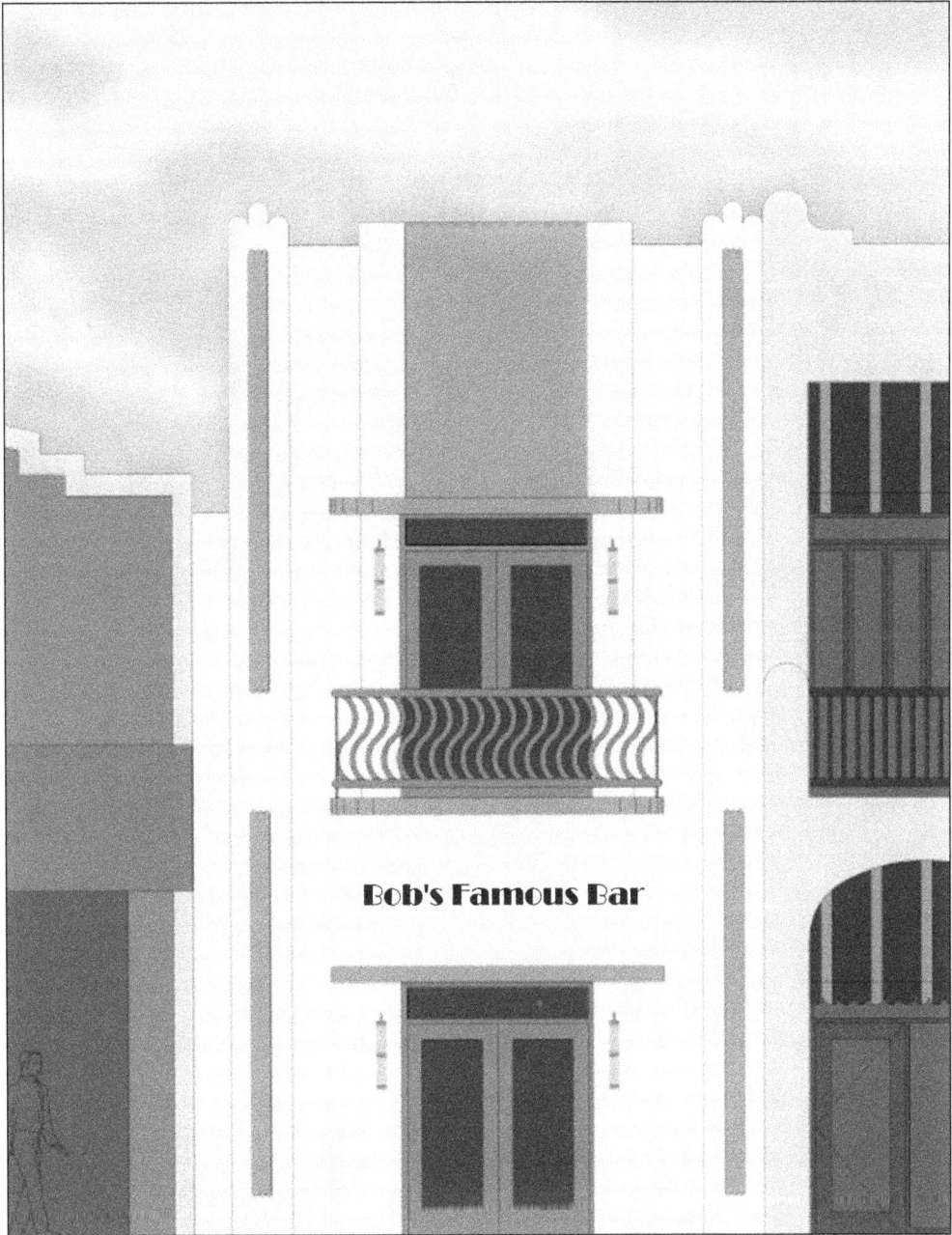

Bob's Famous Bar at 217 East Atlantic Avenue was 100 feet long and 18 feet wide. It was famous for being the longest bar east of the Mississippi. Bob's Famous Bar has a pass-through door that connected to the building on the right (which became Powers Lounge). It was famous for having three things—a bar, a bookie, and a brothel upstairs. Richwagen's Bicycle Shop, in business since 1961, occupied the vertical Art Deco building for 32 years. After both buildings were demolished in 2003, Jess M. Sowards, an architect on the Pineapple Grove Design Committee, created this rendering for the future re-creation of Bob's Famous Bar. This poster reflects an effort to reconstruct architecture that maintains the historic flavor of downtown Delray Beach. (Courtesy of Currie, Sowards, Aguila Architects.)

The J. H. Cousins Dress Shop Building is located at 1220 East Atlantic Avenue one block west of the ocean. Built in 1939 by Gustav Maass, the rounded corners, fluted ribbed columns, eyebrows, bandings, ship-like railings, and interior terrazzo flooring make this building a shining example of Nautical Streamline Moderne architecture. The building, owned by Marion Virginia Cousins, remains in the family.

The geometrical Zig-Zag-style Coral Shores Motel built in the late 1940s is currently a Budget Inn. The motel sits near the Boynton Beach boundary line at 2500 North Federal Highway. The highway parallels the East Coast. It runs 2,390 miles from Key West, Florida, in the South, to Fort Kent, Maine, at the Canadian border in the North.

In 1947, the Seacrest Veterinarian Hospital at 3029 North Federal Highway was built for veterinarian Eric Anderson. Rounded corners and glass-block windows are a shining example of Modernism and technology. Reinforced concrete allowed architects to create modern buildings that were not possible before the Machine Age.

This house at 503 Northeast Second Avenue, just north of Pineapple Grove, is one of the few private residences found in Delray Beach built in the Art Deco style. The building has three stepped-back sections, a flat roof, glass-block windows, rounded eyebrows, and fabulous twin, back-to-back iron gates with a stylized flamingo. See detail on page 105.

This symmetrical detail of the Wenger House exemplifies Art Deco geometry and balance. In this historic treasure, the use of flat linear planes, known as eyebrows, were fanciful and decorative. The eyebrows are assembled like the layers of a wedding cake or a smoke stack. Usually, eyebrows are functional elements placed above windows in order to provide shade from the tropical sun.

In this detail, evenly spaced, stacked, and rounded linear planes follow form as functional steps. The curvilinear staircase swirls around the home, leading to a rooftop environment. The thin railings are reminiscent of the nautical theme, along with the repetition of large and small porthole windows. The historic Wenger House is currently owned by preservationists Linda Stabile and her husband, Calvin Zimmer.

Ruth and Ray Wenger built their home themselves. Construction was completed on the Art Deco dream house in 1948. Ray, shown with his motorcycle, was a jack-of-all-trades, and Ruth was a beautician. Part of the home was built as Ruth's Beauty Salon, with small connecting rooms. In 2006, the Wenger House became the first residence ever to be listed on Palm Beach County's Register of Historic Places.

The Wenger House is a Nautical Moderne private residence built at 3811 Wall Street, in an unincorporated pocket of Palm Beach County. The house is a whimsical fantasy with heart shaped cut-outs in the concrete perimeter enclosure and eyebrows stacked like a wedding cake. In 2000, Boynton Beach artist Rick Beaulieu composed a color scheme for the current owners. (Courtesy of Linda Stabile and Calvin Zimmer.)

In the late 1940s, this Streamline Moderne apartment complex at 90 Southeast Fifth Avenue was built on busy U.S. Highway 1, south of the old Delray Beach Library and Chamber of Commerce. Ten apartments occupy the development that sports eyebrows, a flat roof, glass block, and incised banding details.

Casa del Mar was built near the ocean at 1006 Casuarina Road in the 1940s. The building has straight lines contrasted by a sculptural "wave" that conceals the stairwells on both sides of the long building. In 2004, Art Deco enthusiasts and condominium owners Mace and Sue Comora commissioned Sharon Koskoff to colorize the all-white complex and enhance the architectural elements of the Streamline Moderne apartments.

Three

WONDERS OF LAKE WORTH (CENTRAL COUNTY)

The largest concentration and number (both commercial and residential) of Art Deco buildings in Palm Beach County are found in Lake Worth. The Planning, Zoning, and Historic Preservation Department of the city adopted strong preservation guidelines and ordinances that protect six historic districts within the town. A historic district contains contributing buildings (those with historical significance) and non-contributing buildings (those in the district without historic status).

The Art Deco Society of the Palm Beaches conducts trolley tours of the neighborhood. The tour encompasses the extensive downtown vicinity, the commercial Dixie Highway corridor, and the prominent residential areas. Downtown Lake Worth has two main streets, Lake Avenue (eastward) and Lucerne Avenue (westward), which run to and from the island of Palm Beach. The Lake Worth Playhouse and the Lake Theatre, as seen in chapter one, are the jewels of the historic downtown.

The arts have contributed to a renewed vitality with events such as the Annual Street Painting Festival, chaired by Maryanne Webber and an all-volunteer committee. For two days in February, hundreds of local artists draw pastel masterpieces on closed roadways. The first rainy day washes away the temporary artworks.

The Museum of the City of Lake Worth and the Lake Worth Art League Gallery are located in Old City Hall, now the City Hall Annex at 414 Lake Avenue. In 1989, the annex was listed on the National Register of Historic Places. G. Sherman Childs is Lake Worth's most significant Art Deco architect. He started out as the first draftsman for the famous Addison Mizner, who relied completely on Childs for his architectural drawing skills. Edgar S. Wortman is another notable Lake Worth architect working with Modernism.

Shuffleboard Courts, Lake Worth, Florida

Shuffleboard enjoyed tremendous growth during the early 1900s through the Roaring Twenties. When Prohibition came, speakeasy nightclubs did not need games of skill. Following the repeal of Prohibition, shuffleboard players began to reappear, largely on the East Coast. With little money available for entertainment thanks to the Great Depression, shuffleboard brought out crowds of people. Leagues began to form, and shuffleboard was on the move again.

The Casino at Lake Worth, Florida

The Lake Worth Casino in this 1950s postcard will soon be demolished to make way for contemporary development. It was built in 1948 by the noteworthy architect Edgar S. Wortman. The original Lake Worth Casino was built in 1922 and was designed by G. Sherman Childs. It was battered by several hurricanes and demolished in 1947. Gambling was legal until the mid-1930s, and bathers could enjoy a saltwater swimming pool.

KRISTINES RESTAURANT. 1132 N. DIXIE (U.S. HIGHWAY No. 1) LAKE WORTH. FLA.

Kristine's Restaurant, built in 1945 by Richard Rummell, is located at 1132 North Dixie Highway. It has a fluted, ribbed, futuristic finial shaped like a spaceship, with glass block, neon, and a pyramidal doorway. The letter "K" is incised in the concrete. In 2006, Jetsetter Lounge painted the building purple and lime. It features a swank Tiki Garden, atomic 1960s theme, and "Intergalactic" menu. (Courtesy of Mike Jones.)

Famous Restaurant and Cocktail Lounge was located at 912 Second Avenue. "Where people love to meet" was their slogan. Glass blocks, triangular beams, and a streamlined ceiling made this a modern eatery. The restaurant's interior stayed similar to the postcard until the 1980s, when it was remodeled into the current Palm Beach County–operated senior citizen center.

43

Architect Edgar S. Wortman built two adjacent "twin" Nautical Moderne structures on prime waterfront property in east Lake Worth. The close-up of 810 South Lakeside Drive reveals the northern home (left side) of the pair. The straight lines and cantilever eyebrows parallel Frank Lloyd Wright's famous Fallingwater, Kaufmann House, Pennsylvania, built in 1936.

The home of Edward Martin was built in 1936 at 131 North Lakeside Drive. The private Art Deco residence has rounded corners, three racing-stripe bandings, and glass-block windows. Rectangular incised blocks outline the structure. Original jalousie windows, which are three glass louvers that overlap one another, tilt open, permitting airflow and ventilation.

This Art Deco jewel built in 1939 is the southern home (right side) of the pair built by Wortman at 812 South Lakeside Drive. Located on the Intracoastal Waterway, this 2,000-square-foot private residence features a round, blue Depression glass window. The stepped rooflines and eyebrows reflect the horizontal nature of Florida's flat landscape.

This side entrance detail of 812 South Lakeside Drive is a celebration of horizontal lines. The second floor is stepped back while the functional eyebrows provide needed shade from the hot sun. The rear of the private residence faces South Palm Beach across the Intracoastal Waterway. Samuel H. Ackerman was the building contractor for both homes.

A grand staircase with a semi-circular overhanging eyebrow adorns 401 South Lakeside Drive, a two-level apartment building. The modern structure is located directly across from Bryant Park with its bandshell and boat ramp, built directly on the Intracoastal Waterway. Just north, a drawbridge crosses over to the town of South Palm Beach.

A small and quaint medical office at 220 South O Street sits on the corner lot of Fifth Avenue South. The rounded corner entranceway, roofline banding, and three steps up to the doorway typify the simplicity of Moderne architecture found in this charming commercial structure, built in 1937.

Prominent architect G. Sherman Childs designed this Art Moderne apartment complex at 25 South Lakeside Avenue. The building was appropriately named the Flamingo Apartments for the popular Floridian icon. Childs was one of the first pioneers to move to the city of Lake Worth in the early 1900s. (Courtesy of Tyler Gray.)

Irvin R. Childs (1915–1985) and his sister Irvene were the first twins born in Lake Worth. Irvin owned the curvaceous private residence at 330 South Palmway. He was a navy veteran of World War II, and his wife, Lillian, continued to live in the home until her death in 2004. The twins' father was Lake Worth architect G. Sherman Childs. (Courtesy of Bradley Kane.)

The apartment complex at 230 South Dixie Highway is a medical building with nautical nuances and asymmetrical balance. Two rows of parallel eyebrows divide the building into three horizontal sections. The double doorway placed on the right balances two rectangular shapes that divide the building vertically. Only the left side of the structure has circular cutouts, as detailed below.

A side view of the above building focuses on the repetition of three circular cutouts. On the far right, near the roofline, a circular porthole relief is repeated from the front of the building. The highly geometrical, "boxy" building with its circular punch-outs represents a fascination with the industrialized Machine Age in the 1940s. (Courtesy of Ian Kerner.)

The Seventh Day Adventist Church is located in a residential neighborhood at 701 North Federal Highway. Built in 1940 as a religious institution, it continues today as the Temple Ariel Messianic Congregation. The lightning bolt roofline is a recurring Art Deco architectural element borrowed from other historically geometrical styles such as Egyptian, Mayan, and Aztec.

This close-up photograph of the Seventh Day Adventist Church highlights the circular fluted, ribbed columns and the entranceway of the spiritual institution. The two porthole windows and three rectangular inscribed stripes appear to be a smiling face. This hall is a mere 2,000 square feet. (Courtesy of Ryan Kerner.)

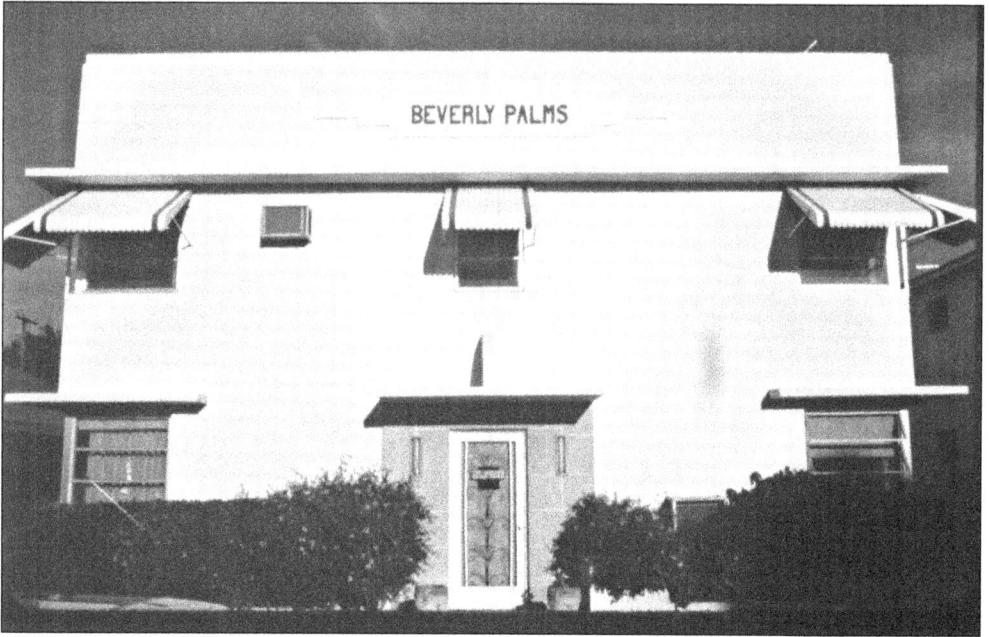

The Beverly Palms is located at 118 South Lakeside Drive. An uninterrupted eyebrow stretches across the second story. Permanent and retractable metal awnings adorn the upper-floor windows, providing decoration and shade from the tropical sun. The horizontal flat roof and symmetrical quality of the building are prime examples of Modernism.

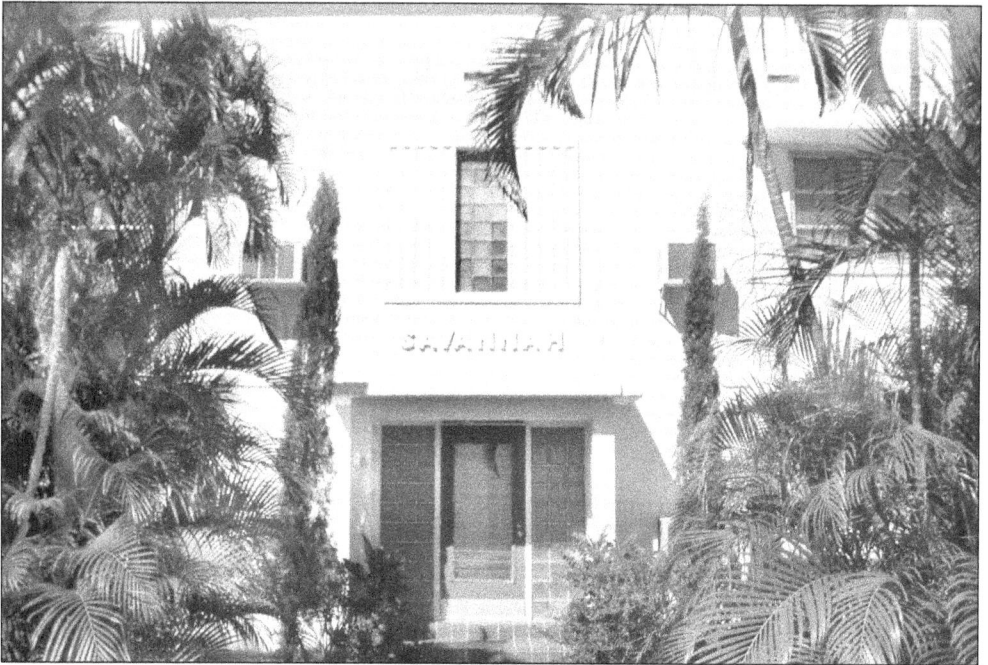

The Savannah multifamily dwelling was built at 101 South Lakeside Drive by Arthur L. Weeks in the late 1940s. Behind the lush foliage, a modern facade is revealed. A fluted ribbed relief frames a glass-block skylight. The eyebrows over the windows and entranceway are constructed in a Zig-Zag formation. The name of the building is delicately embossed in capital letters.

Carolyn Apartments was built by Edgar S. Wortman in the late 1940s at 23 South Lakeside Drive. This minimal building has a flat roof and fluted ribbing atop the main entrance. A contrasting perpendicular plane, vertically placed creating a right angle, intersects the circular eyebrow above the door.

The Phil-Mar apartment complex squarely sits at 111 South Lakeside sheltered by dense landscaping. The multifamily dwelling is U-shaped, and its ultra-straight lines are reminiscent of the German Bauhaus style. Two columns of single glass block resemble double-breasted "buttons" on a sailor's shirt. The only rounded lines are the eyebrows and the second-floor landing.

The Art Shop, at 705 Lucerne Avenue, celebrated their 50th anniversary in 2006. It is the oldest surviving business in downtown Lake Worth. Lucy and Dick Purnell ran the shop from 1961 until 1985. Maryanne and Bruce Webber purchased the gallery spaces and during a 1990s renovation added cornices to the marquee, replicating the original centerpieces found on the Art Deco structure. (Courtesy of Maryanne and Bruce Webber Galleries.)

The Lake Palm Apartment complex at 112 Lake Avenue houses 10 units. The single elongated building is sliced in two by a *via*-like patio walkway. The strong horizontal lines are reinforced by its flat roof and surrounding eyebrows. Arthur L. Weeks built this Streamline Moderne building in the late 1940s.

The Deshon Apartments, at 101 South J Street, is one of Lake Worth's largest Streamline Moderne apartment buildings. Navy-blue rows of banding are made of pigmented sculptural glass called Vitrolite. Used predominantly for wall surfacing, it revolutionized the architectural glass industry and rapidly became a favorite medium of architects and designers. The veneer material can be cut, laminated, curved, colored, or illuminated for exterior and interior surfaces.

This photograph is a front view of the Lake Palm Apartments as shown on the opposite page. Technology now allowed windows to be "cantilevered" or mitered without the corner support of a load-bearing wall. Decorative brick-face as ornamentation around the doorway is a tribute to Northern buildings and a contrast to the customary stucco used in South Florida.

53

The historic Art Moderne structure at 1001 North Federal Highway sits on girders in 2006. The property is a designated contributing building in the Northeast Lucerne Local Historic District. The dwelling sat midway on a lot, and developers wanted to demolish it. The solution was to move the building and design three-story townhouses around it. The protected historic structure will be used as a clubhouse, pool cabana, and meeting room.

The 101 House on Lucerne Avenue consists of four efficiencies and a clerestory gallery living room. Just west of the Intracoastal Waterway Bridge at Lakeside Drive, it was the first air-conditioned apartment building in Palm Beach County. Built by local contractor and owner Samuel H. Ackerman in 1938, the 101 House was considered the "City's Most Modernistic Apartments." Original blue Depression glass continues to adorn the two-story windows on the left.

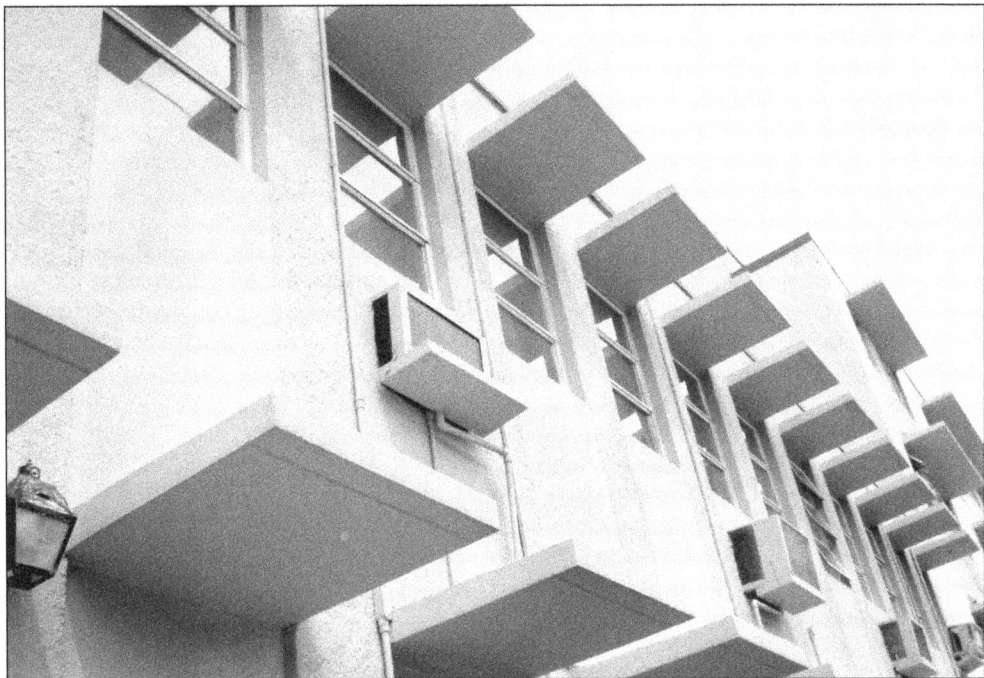

A detail of the Crest Manor nursing home, located at 504 Third Avenue, displays a pattern of remarkable individual eyebrows over each window. During a remodeling phase to become an assisted living facility, unexplained presences and happenings were reported by construction workers and security guards. It is rumored that the souls of former patients, unable to rest after death, were the cause.

The Blue Marlin Bar, built in the 1940s, was a popular nightspot and favorite hangout among locals for decades. Located on the main drag at 1101 North Dixie Highway, the building is now vacant and available for rent. Fresh paint and restoration highlight the vertical planes with triple diamond-shaped cutouts on the right.

The A. G. Holley State Hospital was opened in 1950 as the Southeast Tuberculosis Hospital, on Lantana Road, south of the city of Lake Worth. Reynolds, Smith and Hills, Inc., was the engineering, architectural design, and environmental services contractor. A. G. Holley Hospital serves as Florida's only public health hospital and is the last of the original American sanatoriums. Currently operating, it is dedicated primarily to the cure of tuberculosis and is an integral part of the Department of Health, Division of Disease Control. The Streamline Moderne building, with 162,000 square feet, is the largest Art Deco structure in the state. Unfortunately the building's exterior was neglected and it has deteriorated. It is slated to be demolished and redeveloped, although preservationists and concerned community activists are desperately working to save it. Shown are the vertical glass-block entryway and the full structure in its original splendor.

New Southeast Florida State Sanatorium
Lantana, Palm Beach County, Florida.

Four

HISTORIC WEST PALM BEACH (NORTH COUNTY)

The urban city of West Palm Beach was founded by Henry Flagler in 1894. It was designed as a community to house the servants working in the two grand hotels of neighboring Palm Beach, the Royal Poinciana Hotel and the Breakers Hotel. During the 1920s, the city boomed, leaving it with many historic structures and neighborhoods that create a rich sense of time and place.

The two most prolific Art Deco architects found in the city of West Palm Beach are William Manly King (institutional structures) and Belford Washington "Wren" Shoumate (residential mansions).

In 1988, the City of West Palm Beach became involved in historic preservation, conducted a survey of its architectural treasures, and adopted a Historic Preservation Ordinance. Fifteen historic districts were designated, and eight were placed on the National Register of Historic Places.

In the late 1980s, a planning project called Uptown/Downtown demolished hundreds of old and historic buildings along the Okeechobee Boulevard corridor. The city's gateway remained vacant until 2001 when CityPlace was built in the retro Mediterranean style. It has since become a successful shopping and entertainment district.

Attracting crowds since 1995, Clematis by Night sizzles every Thursday to a popular concert series at the Centennial Square Fountain. The Clematis Street Historic Commercial District is on the National Register of Historic Places. It is filled with nightclubs, restaurants, and the West Palm Beach Library. Free trolley rides shuttle passengers between CityPlace and Clematis Street.

Band Stand in Flagler Park, West Palm Beach, Florida

The bandstand in Flagler Park, named for oil and railroad magnate Henry Morrison Flagler, has always been an important public space in West Palm Beach. The city created a variation at the eastern end of Clematis Street, where two angled, short streets branched off to create a triangular, public common area, formerly City Park. The bandstand attracted thousands during the warm winter months.

Radio Station WJNO, West Palm Beach, Florida

Photo by George Sanderson

WJNO Radio Station in West Palm Beach was on the Intracoastal Waterway, one block north of the Flagler Bridge. WJNO signed on at 1:00 p.m. on July 31, 1936. Originally a CBS affiliate, it aired everything from classical music to comedian Steve Allen. By the 1940s, over 90 percent of all radio listeners from Palm Beach to Lake Worth were tuned to WJNO (1200 AM), the only signal between Orlando and Miami.

The Triangle Club, an Alcoholics Anonymous meeting place, was housed in a 1938 building at 423 Fourth Street. Sharon Koskoff was commissioned to design a color restoration of white, teal, and rust in the early 1990s. The building was endangered, and the restoration added value to the structure. Several years later, when the Nautical Moderne building was demolished, the group had enough capital to move to a new home.

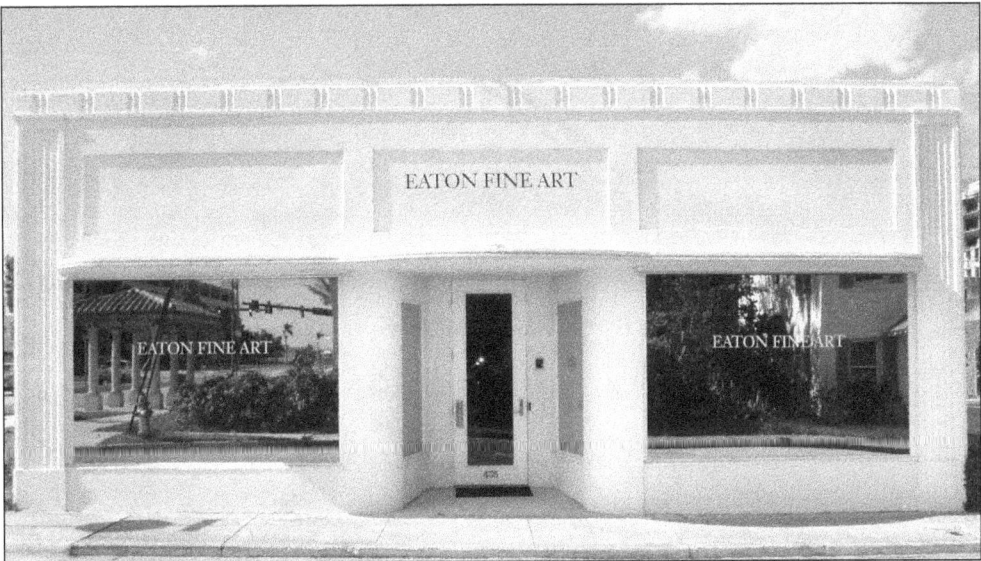

Lainhart and Potter Hardware, 435 Gardenia Street, was built in 1941. It was named for George W. Lainhart, who sold construction materials to Henry Flagler for his railroads and hotels. In 1995, Timothy Andrew Eaton, of Eaton Fine Art, renovated the historic Art Moderne facility. A north gallery addition and an adjacent sculpture garden, designed by Mary Anna Eaton, complement the gallery of Nineteenth and Twentieth Century American and European fine art.

The West Palm Beach Chamber of Commerce, demolished in the early 1990s, was built at 501 North Flagler Drive. The Art Moderne civic building has stepped-back columns with Zig-Zag cornices. An eyebrow is centrally located over the doors of the symmetrical edifice. A new chamber, built by Peacock and Lewis at 401 North Flagler, was built in the Post Modern style with a full-length circular glass-block wall.

Selby Shoes, at 207 Clematis Street, features rectangular display windows and a bold aluminum banding. The use of machine-inspired industrial design was especially popular with commercial buildings for the marketing of products. The movement and acceleration of a passing locomotive is suggested. The modern essence of the building has now been lost and remodeled into a Spanish cuisine restaurant, Maison Carlos.

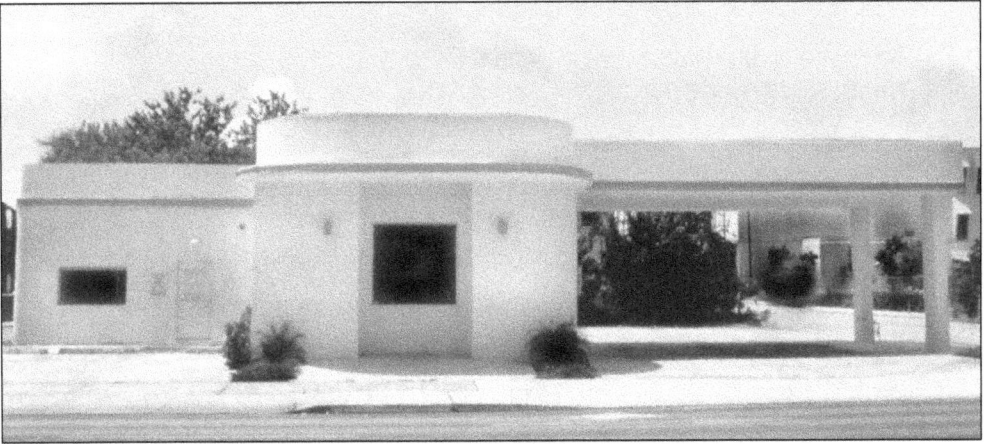

Belford Shoumate, the Palm Beaches' most significant residential Modernist architect, also built several commercial bus stations around the county in the early 1930s. The Trailways Building, located at 501 South Olive Avenue, is one that still stands. Trailways was a system of privately owned motorcoach companies working together to increase passenger traffic, safety, and convenience. Attorney-at-law Matthew S. Nugent owned and occupied the building from 1985 until 2004.

Lloyd Bell Appliances, built in 1935, became the Elephants Foot Antiques Shop. The flat roof, sleek row of bandings, and rounded corners made this building a treasure. In 1986, it was the first Streamline Moderne building identified and listed on the Art Deco Society of the Palm Beaches Historic Register. It was located at 310 South Olive Avenue, demolished in the 1990s, and is currently a senior residence parking lot.

North of downtown West Palm Beach and tucked away from the waterfront is a reemerging community steeped in architectural history. The private residence at 2813 Poinsettia Avenue, built in 1946 for Spartaco Castiglioni, is in the Old Northwood Historic District. North Dixie Highway becomes Poinsettia Avenue after Twenty-fifth Street, the start of the up-and-coming district.

The Ulysses and Marion Ridley House is a two-story private residence at 822 Fifteenth Street at Division Street. It is a contributing building to the Northwest Historic District. In February 1992, the area became West Palm Beach's first of eight historic districts to be included on the National Register of Historic Places.

At 2500 Broadway, the Sunset Grill is a restaurant in a sleek Streamline Moderne structure with eyebrows, flat roof, and rounded corners. The parapet of the stucco tavern has three steps down on both sides, while the eyebrow wraps around the corner. Built in 1940, the structure, located in the Northwood Village Shopping District, is enjoying a thriving cultural renaissance.

The Robinson House, built in 1925, is the oldest residence listed on the Art Deco Society of the Palm Beaches Historic Register. Carl and Maude Robinson, who were of African American descent, operated grocery stores. Located at 720 Fifteenth Street in the Northwest Historic District, the house was built by Albert Williams. Vertical fluted ribbing and banding are replicated on the first and stepped-back second floors.

Mounts Botanical Gardens displays tropical plants from around the world. It is Palm Beach County's oldest and largest public garden. Located at 531 North Military Trail, Mounts is three miles west of downtown. It was built in 1954 by architect George Votaw. The building represents a transitional period of architecture into Mid-Century Modern.

The Coleman Funeral Home at 1215 Tamarind Avenue is located just south of Palm Beach Lakes Boulevard. The early structure, built in 1929, reveals three brick columns supporting a connecting eyebrow. A stepped-back ornament breaks the line of the flat roof. Individual eyebrows overhang each window. Both glass-block windows are framed by decorative borders of irregular shaped stone-face.

The Peninsular Plumbing Company Warehouse, at 501 Fern Street, has been the home of John C. Cassidy Air Conditioning for over 40 years. The white building was constructed in 1938 by Patterson-Strong contractors. In the industrial neighborhood north of Okeechobee Boulevard, the streets are named alphabetically for native flora, hence Banyan, Clematis, Datura, Evernia, Fern, Gardenia, Hibiscus, and Iris.

Built in 1943, this multifamily dwelling at 215 Conniston Road, at Washington Road, lies across from the Intracoastal Waterway. Just north of Southern Boulevard, the apartment building has incised bandings that surround the U-shaped perimeter. Eyebrows, flat roof, and a stepped-back roofline add to the Streamline Moderne elements of the building.

Belford Shoumate was the architect for the Elmer and Laura Shopp House, built in 1940. The two-story private residence with balconies is prominently located at 3135 Washington Road, beside other substantial mansions. The rounded front entrance overhang is nautically designed, and the wrought-iron gate has three non-concentric circles above vertical stylized waves. An interior detail is shown on page 106.

This is the back cottage of 140 Monroe Drive, shown on the opposite page. Many homes in West Palm Beach have additional quarters in the rear. The rounded entrance, swirling eyebrow, and flat roof resemble the nautical main house, also built by Belford Shoumate. The private residence is located one block west of the Intracoastal Waterway. (Courtesy of Jean and Sumner Draper.)

The Victor and Eleanor Barbour House is currently owned by Jean and Sumner Draper, who restored the house and property. Belford Shoumate built the home at 140 Monroe Drive in 1933. This multilevel home has a stepped, rounded entrance with yellow and navy-blue Vitrolite banding. The working fireplace chimney imitates the smokestack of an ocean liner. (Courtesy of Jean and Sumner Draper.)

The rear of the Barbour House shows off its maritime characteristics. The elongated staircase must be straddled while facing the building, more like a ship's ladder than a staircase. On the roof's landing is a studio with built-in furniture and shelving, as if to avoid the rolling seas. The Drapers have hosted several parties for the Art Deco Society of the Palm Beaches' members. (See page 120.) (Courtesy of Jean and Sumner Draper.)

The Ralph and Edna Wagner House, at 2631 South Flagler Drive, faces east, toward the Intracoastal Waterway and the island of Palm Beach. This drawing is the original sketch created by Ralph Wagner, an engineer, of his dream house to be designed by architect Belford Shoumate. The following six photographs will show how Wagner's concept became a reality and an Art Deco masterpiece. (Courtesy of Cheryl and Homer Marshman.)

Cheryl and Homer Marshman are the current owners of the Wagner House, built in 1937. Their entrance has two vertical reliefs of stylized floral and water patterns that repeat throughout the house. The protruding curved entranceway, with simplified scroll-like waves, drape like a stage curtain. Two oversized porthole windows look out to the Intracoastal Waterway. Additional details are discussed in chapter seven. (Courtesy of Cheryl and Homer Marshman.)

The facade of the two-story residence closely resembles the original sketch. The Wagner House is the largest Art Deco luxury mansion in West Palm Beach. Bas-relief, circular windows, columns, and elongated arched windows identify this house as the most formal and opulent on the historic register. In 1999, a sensitive expansion provided a guesthouse, garage, and a stucco perimeter wall by architectural group Zeidler Roberts Partnership. (Courtesy of Cheryl and Homer Marshman.)

This magnificent home has a grand pool and patio area to match. The open rounded railings add a nautical feel to the outdoor swimming pool area. On the left are stepped ledges with wave-like swirls. The architectural motif reappears as ornamentation throughout the exterior as well as the interior of the house. (Courtesy of Cheryl and Homer Marshman.)

This view of the private residence at 2631 South Flagler Drive is the southward side as seen from Belmonte Road. It defines the chimney of the functioning fireplace that graces the main first-floor living room. The vertical architectural column has a stylized floral relief and stepped-back sides. The Wagner House is a contributing historic building in the El Cid Historic District of West Palm Beach. The district is listed on the National Register of Historic Places. (Courtesy of Cheryl and Homer Marshman.)

An original interior photograph of the Wagner House outlines an arched corridor with three circular "steps" at the ceiling line. The far end of the photograph reveals the north side entrance of the sitting room lobby. The high ceilings were a symbol of luxury, comfort, and exuberance in earlier days just after the Great Depression. The triple arched windows on the right are mirrored by the doorways on the left. The spacious passageway leads to other entertainment rooms with a fireplace, built-in bar, and family rooms. The modern furniture is reflected in the comfortable overstuffed chairs that are straight-lined, rectangular, and without embellishment. (Courtesy of Cheryl and Homer Marshman.)

Another original interior photograph of the Wagner House on South Flagler Drive highlights the grand staircase up to the second level. The flooring is made of polished terrazzo, consisting of marble chips set in epoxy resin that is poured and ground smooth when dry. Terrazzo was ubiquitous to South Florida and modern design. It has high-class elegance, hard-wearing properties, and

keeps the floor cool amidst the tropical heat. The pilaster (a column attached to the wall) reaches to the ceiling next to the powder room door. As shown on the left, the chairs are masculine in nature with squared backs. A large chair in the foreground has tight vertical tufting. (Courtesy of Cheryl and Homer Marshman.)

The Rinker Residence stands on the waterfront at 2111 South Flagler Drive. In 1925, Marshall Edison "Doc" Rinker, an Indiana native, moved to Florida and started Rinker Rock and Sand. The company later became Rinker Materials, Inc., one of the largest ready-mix concrete and block producers in the country. Maurice Fatio, a famed Palm Beach architect who designed several Art Moderne structures, built this house in 1938.

Fatio designed the rear poolside of the Rinker Residence with a corner of glass block looking into the living room. He had a reputation for being a "society architect." He mingled with the inner circles, and his clients ranged from the Vanderbilts to the Rockefellers. This neighborhood features some of the city's largest and most elaborately designed historic homes and is associated with jogging and biking trails. (Courtesy of M. G. Owens.)

Five

NAUTICAL PALM BEACH (THE ISLAND)

The barrier island of Palm Beach is world-renowned for its extraordinary beauty, cosmopolitan attitude, and small-town character. Worth Avenue is filled with legendary international boutiques, upscale merchants, and specialty stores that are distinguished by Old-World charm. Although Palm Beach has only a handful of Art Deco structures, each one is a prized gem.

Belford Shoumate is the most popular architect of Modernism featured on the 16-mile-long island. On November 2, 1989, Sharon Koskoff met with Belford Shoumate and his wife, Betsy, in their Phipps Plaza residential offices. Belford answered questions and spoke of the Golden Age of Palm Beach architecture. He worked with Joseph Urban, a theatrical designer and architect, on the Paramount Theatre and the Mar-A-Lago mansion in Palm Beach.

The Preservation Foundation of Palm Beach houses the Jack C. Massey Architectural Archives in the heart of town at 311 Peruvian Avenue. It contains the complete architectural drawing collections that belonged to Belford Shoumate (Art Deco mansions), Wyeth, King and Johnson (Norton Gallery and Museum of Art), and Henry Harding.

Notable residents of Palm Beach, past and present, include real estate developer Donald Trump, Post cereal heiress Marjorie Merriweather Post, Wall Street broker E. F. Hutton, the political Kennedy family, and the cosmetic Estée Lauder family.

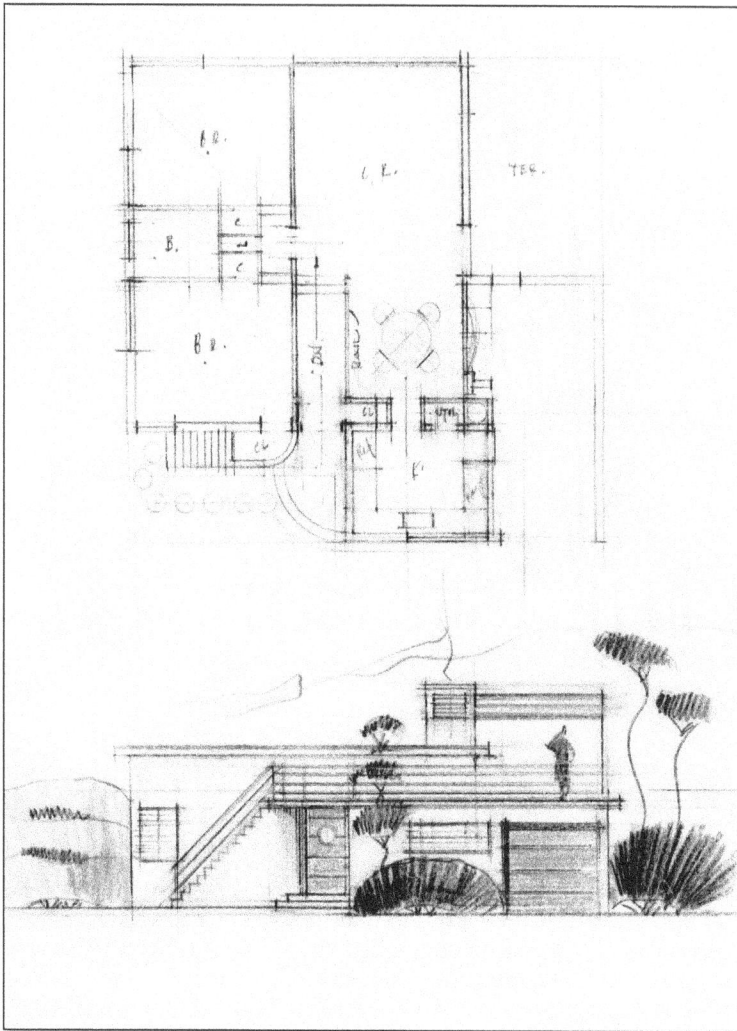

In the 1930s, Belford Shoumate created these unidentified sketches on vellum of Art Deco structures in Palm Beach. In this original sketch, both the floor plan and the facade of the nautical home are included. The Preservation Foundation of Palm Beach is the sole beneficiary for thousands of his architectural drawings and other archival materials, including blueprints, photographs, and slides. (Courtesy of Preservation Foundation of Palm Beach.)

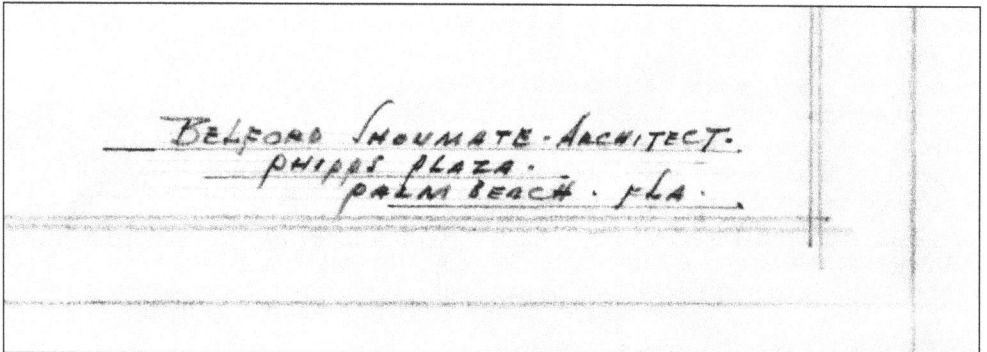

Belford Shoumate studied architecture at the University of Pennsylvania and graduated in 1930. He is listed in Who's Who in America. Belford and his wife, Betsy, had two sons, William "Tec" Stanford Shoumate and Thomas Stanford Shoumate. Belford's sons continue in the tradition of their father with Shoumate Construction, on the mainland of West Palm Beach. (Courtesy of Preservation Foundation of Palm Beach.)

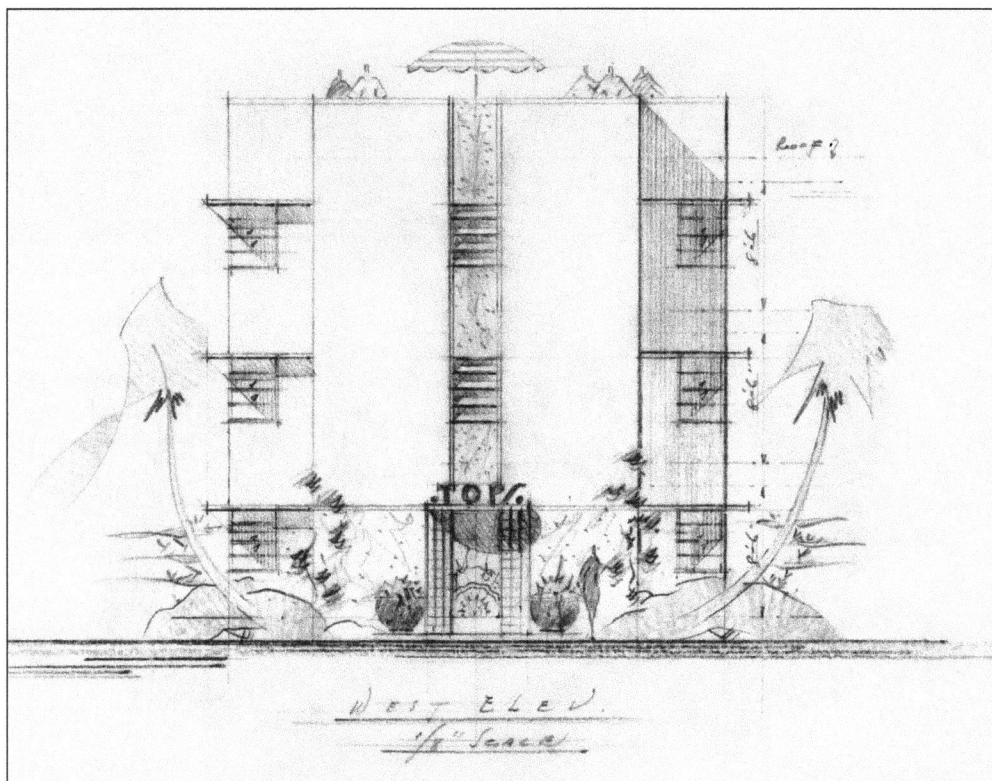

This unfamiliar rendering of "Tops" clearly announces Shoumate's interest and skill in modernity as he strays from the very dominant Mediterranean Revival style that reigned over Palm Beach in the 1930s. The building illustrates various fundamentals of Art Deco architecture such as the flat roof, eyebrows, use of threes, bandings, glass block, symmetry, corner mitered windows, and central verticality. (Courtesy of Preservation Foundation of Palm Beach.)

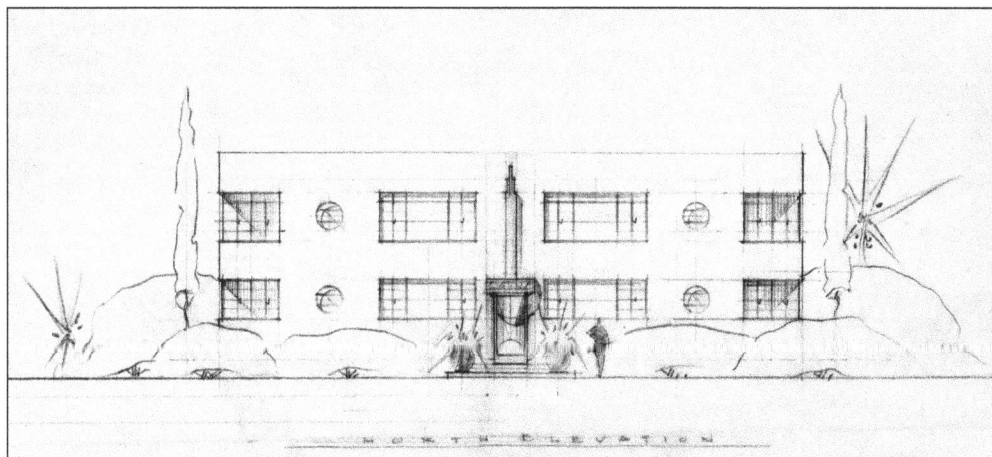

This mysterious drawing concentrates on horizontal elements that are associated with Nautical Moderne buildings in Palm Beach. The Atlantic Ocean on the east and the Intracoastal Waterway on the west mirror the building's mass. Shoumate's circular porthole windows, flat roof, and a Zig-Zag vertical finial atop the entranceway master the understanding and aesthetics of Maritime Modernism. (Courtesy of Preservation Foundation of Palm Beach.)

Belford Washington "Wren" Shoumate, portrayed at age 27, was one of eight siblings who were descendants from the Cherokee Nation, Shawnee Tribe. He was born in Aberdeen, Ohio, on June 5, 1903, and was raised in Mobile, Alabama. For 54 years, Shoumate worked from his Palm Beach home office in Phipps Plaza, known as Architects Row. Belford died on his 88th birthday in 1991. (Courtesy of Preservation Foundation of Palm Beach.)

Belford Shoumate's original sketch, identified by the Art Deco Society of the Palm Beaches as the 1221 North Lake Way nautical mansion, is shown in the following nine photographs. The 6,000-square-foot home sits on the northwest end of the island on the Intracoastal Waterway, with eastern beachfront access and a cabana. (Courtesy of Preservation Foundation of Palm Beach.)

The front entrance of the Fore and Aft House, built in 1937, is unassuming and discreet. Rumors claim the house was awarded "House of the Future" during the 1939 New York World's Fair. On the right, an entry door houses two cars that can drive in and out of a Y-shaped garage with two individual exits. Futuristic innovations make this house a product of the "World of Tomorrow," part of the 1939 World's Fair . (Courtesy of Kirby Kooluris.)

The curvilinear rear view or "aft" looks like a land-locked ocean liner with its Art Deco railings and rounded corners. The pool is shaped like a musical note, a whimsical element that is repeated in other areas of the nautical three-story home. A third-floor outdoor deck faces west onto the Intracoastal Waterway, providing remarkable sunsets. (Courtesy of Kirby Kooluris.)

The south side elevation of 1221 North Lake Way has repeating concrete columns and a second entrance directly to the living room. This view of the house shows the nautical upper deck with steamship railings. The concrete columns each have three porthole cutouts. This Belford Shoumate house is a tribute to the speed of modern travel and global transportation.

Kirby Kooluris owned the streamlined house from 1982 until 2001. The following interior photographs were taken in 1988 after he completely restored the house. The bright living room is shown with the original furniture and an extra-large circular window facing the south. Squared-off sofa chairs sit diagonally in the living room, which has hosted Art Deco Society of the Palm Beaches membership events. (Courtesy of Kirby Kooluris.)

Kirby's great uncle, Nathan Dolinsky, painted the original canvas above the fireplace. Dolinsky (1890–1981) exhibited his figurative oil paintings at the Armory Show of New York in 1913. He also created four large-scale murals—*Spring, Summer, Fall,* and *Winter*—which were hung in the entrance hallway. A concealed vertical closet hides built-in bookshelves. (Courtesy of Kirby Kooluris.)

An upstairs bathroom, one of five, is a dramatic Shoumate design of bright yellow tile with black trim. The circular-shaped mirror is replicated in negative space with a window in the shower. The porthole catches the ocean breeze that circulates airflow throughout. Fore and Aft has five bedrooms, each with their own exterior entrance that opens individually, like the staterooms of an ocean liner. (Courtesy of Kirby Kooluris.)

The 1221 North Lake Way house has a self-contained kitchen, re-creating another ship-like quality. Access from the living area to the kitchen is up three steps and down three steps. This barrier design is a common element found in floating vessels. If water leaks into an area, the steps restrain the floodwaters from spilling over into the next compartment. (Courtesy of Kirby Kooluris.)

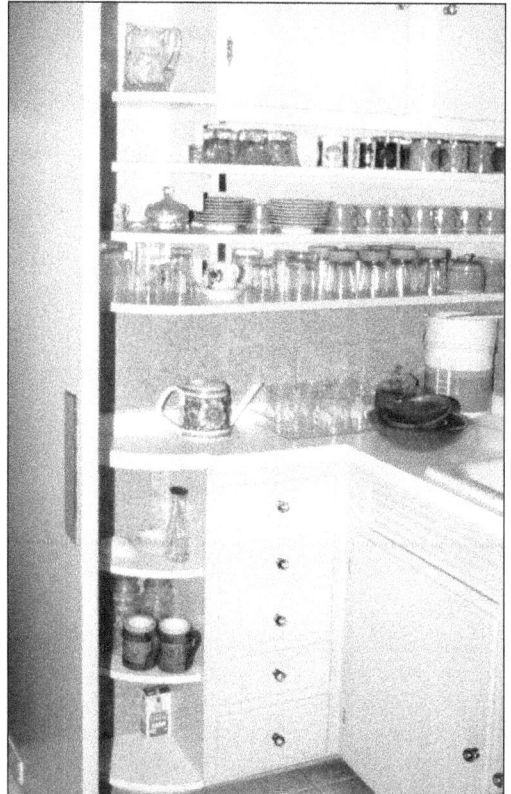

The kitchen or "galley" was built for ultimate modern convenience. Three open shelves provide quick and easy access for setting the table and entertaining. The streamlined kitchen, built for speed, has three-tiered shelving that looks like eyebrows or architectural bandings. The knobs of the draws are made of round translucent glass in aqua-blue, a favorite color in maritime design. (Courtesy of Kirby Kooluris.)

The small eat-in kitchen that seats four is one of the most photographed Art Deco rooms of the Shoumate masterpiece. The ceiling has a Zig-Zag stepped profile. The pyramid shape is repeated in the built-in shelves on the far wall that display wine glasses and a cocktail shaker. The silhouettes of the wooden chair backs emulate the same Zig-Zag stepped motif as the sides of the table. The legs of the chairs and table follow a stepped-back column design. Green glass serves as the tabletop. The uncomplicated lighting is a triangular nautical globe. The burl maple parquet flooring throughout the house was restored to its original splendor. The house was one of the first Art Deco residences to be designated as a historical landmark in Palm Beach. (Courtesy of Kirby Kooluris.)

In 1945, Maurice "Buster" or "Bus" Holley built the Art Moderne private residence at 240 Atlantic Avenue in Palm Beach (not to be confused with Atlantic Avenue in Delray Beach). Holley (1905–1969) also designed the Colony Hotel and Bustani Building in Palm Beach. The 1,000-square-foot structure stands hidden behind bushes, amidst large Mediterranean Revival mansions, on the north side of the street.

The Leonardo is just to the west, at 246 Atlantic Avenue. The apartment building has applied brick that adorns the entranceway in a Zig-Zag pattern. Double rows of glass block act as sidelights, framing the door. A single eyebrow hangs over the glass-paned door. The house, built in the 1940s, has elegance and symmetry.

The treasure located at 150 Australian Avenue was built in the early 1940s. The house is situated several blocks north of Worth Avenue, Palm Beach's world-famous shopping district. The structure is similar in character to the Leonardo but has a full curtain of glass block on the second story. Green incised stripes streamline the design. The structure has been completely restored, and wooden shutters have been added.

The Water Pumping Station on North Lake Way is located in the Coral Cut Historic District. The horizontal building was designed by John Volk, who was one of several architects who made their reputations designing lavish homes and hotels in the Florida land boom of the 1920s. Volk was born in Graz, Austria, and lived in Palm Beach until he died at the age of 82 in February 1984.

In 1937, Shoumate designed the Sam Davis House at 162 Peruvian Avenue. Railings along the roof are reminiscent of an ocean liner. This home features five cutout ring shapes on the left side that reflect the Machine Age. Inside, a blue Depression glass porthole skylight retracts from the ceiling. The Town of Palm Beach designated the house a landmark in 1992, when it was occupied by Michele Wood.

The Reef is an oceanfront masterpiece built for Mr. and Mrs. Vadim Makaroff by architects Treanor and Fatio in 1936. The 2.5-acre estate at 702 North County Road faces the blue Atlantic, on a lot secluded from distractions by privacy gates and landscaping. Two corner projections on the symmetrical house make this seaworthy architectural achievement the best design of Maurice Fatio's career. (Courtesy of Preservation Foundation of Palm Beach/Alexandra Fatio Taylor.)

Maurice Fatio won a gold medal award at the 1937 Paris Exposition for The Reef. He followed Le Corbusier's five points of architecture: flat rooftop gardens, free-plane facade, subdivided space, long horizontal windows, and *piloti* columns to elevate the mass off the ground. The landmarked home was saved from demolition in 1990 by the Palm Beach Landmarks Preservation Commission. (Courtesy of Preservation Foundation of Palm Beach/Alexandra Fatio Taylor.)

An interior photograph of the internationally acclaimed home, The Reef exposes a 29-foot horizontal window looking out onto 200 feet of ocean property. The style of sophisticated French minimalist designer Jean-Michel Frank adorns the living room, library, and dining room. The 16,550-square-foot dream home includes amenities such as a heated pool, movie theater, bowling alley, tennis court, and pavilion. (Courtesy of Preservation Foundation of Palm Beach/Alexandra Fatio Taylor.)

Paramount Building, Palm Beach, Florida

The Paramount Theatre, located at 130 North County Road, was built by theatrical architect Joseph Urban. He was also Marjorie Merriweather Post's architect for Mar-A-Lago. The Paramount Theatre, built in 1927, is correctly identified as Moorish Deco, although it is often mistaken for Mediterranean Revival. This postcard depicts multiple flat roofs that step up and a triangular floor plan one-fourth in scale to that of Urban's Art Deco Radio City Music Hall. (Courtesy of Preservation Foundation of Palm Beach.)

The Little Stark Club, a successful Art Moderne cocktail lounge and package store next to the Biltmore Hotel, was built after Prohibition. It was located at 162 Bradley Place, named for Col. Edward Riley Bradley, a respected churchman and philanthropist. He operated the nation's longest-running illegal gambling establishment for over 50 years, called the Beach Club. It had one of the most expensive and swanky restaurants in the world.

Surfside Hotel, "Just off the ocean," Palm Beach, Florida

The independent Surfside Hotel, 130 Hammon Avenue, was across from the larger Colony Hotel. It was purchased and operated as their satellite. During the 1960s, security for the Kennedy administration stayed at the Surfside. In the 1970s, it was demolished to create the Colony Hotel parking lot. The Colony Hotel is famous for hosting American presidents and European royalty. (Courtesy of the Preservation Foundation of Palm Beach.)

C. 17—Entrance to Popular Pier at Palm Beach, Florida

In the 1940s, the Palm Beach Pier extended Worth Avenue directly over the water, stretching more than 200 feet into the Atlantic Ocean. It featured a bait shop and restaurant that had an old-fashioned soda counter with stools. Open until 4:00 a.m., the pier's restaurant attracted an eclectic mix of late-night merrymakers and early-morning anglers. In 1966, the pier was damaged in a storm and later demolished. (Courtesy of the Preservation Foundation of Palm Beach.)

Originally, the Plaza Inn at 215 Brazilian Avenue, built in 1940, was known as the Ardma Hotel. The architect was Lake Worth's G. Sherman Childs, and the builder was Howard E. Merrill. The Art Deco jewel is open during the winter months. All 48 rooms in the historic boutique hotel are individually decorated.

F. S. Henemader Antiques and Hamburger Heaven, at 316 and 314 South County Road, share a Streamline Moderne building. The rounded corner wraps around to Brazilian Avenue just east of the historic Plaza Inn. The aerodynamic structure emphasizes speed and travel as cars stream by on the commercial street. F. S. Henemader sells French and English antiques. Hamburger Heaven has been serving the "world's best burgers" and desserts since 1945.

Six

OUTER LIMITS (WESTERN PALM BEACH AND MARTIN COUNTIES)

Outer Limits is devoted to Art Deco architecture found in two historic areas other than the eastern seaboard of Palm Beach County.

The first area is the Glades region of western Palm Beach County. Cities include Canal Point, Pahokee, and Belle Glade, on the southern shores of Lake Okeechobee, the second-largest freshwater lake within the continental United States. Agriculture is the number-one industry, as the soil is perfect for growing sugarcane and vegetables. Ironically the Art Deco buildings of the region remain because there is a low rate of new development. Many of these structures are deteriorating because of lack of funds, poor maintenance, and damage from hurricanes.

The Lawrence E. Will Museum, at 530 South Main Street, is owned by the City of Belle Glade and is operated by the Palm Beach County Library District. Their mission is to collect, conserve, and display historical artifacts pertinent to Lake Okeechobee and the upper Everglades.

The second area is Martin County, Palm Beach County's northern cousin on the Treasure Coast. The city of Stuart is located on the Port St. Lucie River. It supports a Florida Main Street Program that works to revitalize the state's historic resources located in traditional commercial centers. Stuart celebrates the 20th anniversary of its Dancin' in the Streets music festival in August 2007.

The Historical Society of Martin County is located in the Elliott Museum at 825 Northeast Ocean Boulevard. The museum contains art galleries, the Country Store, and a world-renowned car gallery including the oldest Cadillac in the country.

The Art Deco Martin County Courthouse is home of the Martin County Council of the Arts and is showcased on page 22.

A parade proudly marches on West Avenue A in downtown Belle Glade in 1947. The black veterans' unit displays the banner of "Earl William Mayes" from the American Legion Post 202, purportedly the largest African American unit in Florida. In the background of the photograph, the procession marches past the Art Moderne Glades Five-and-Dime Store with its Zig-Zag roofline. (Courtesy of the Lawrence E. Will Museum.)

L. W. Armstrong, D.D.S., Pahokee's first farmer, arrived on February 28, 1915. This 1932 photograph shows the dental office and the Bank of Pahokee. The office was completed just before the infamous hurricane of September 1928. The Red Cross used the building for its headquarters following the storm that killed approximately 2,500 people. Mrs. Armstrong's new 1932 Buick is parked out front. (Courtesy of Ann O'Connell Rust/Alvin Armstrong.)

The former Belle Glade Fire Department is located on the 100 block of West Avenue A. To the east is the former Belle Glade City Hall built by William Manly King. The Belle Glade Police Department, behind the fire department, was in use until 2004. The first fire engine truck, bought in 1931, was a used 1913 chain driver. The second fire engine, the "pumper," was bought new in 1936.

Another photograph of the Belle Glade parade displays transportation. The West Palm Beach assistant fire chief officially rides in the front sedan followed by the Belle Glade Fire Department's pumper. The current district fire chief of Palm Beach County, Stephen R. Rice, still uses the vintage fire truck for parades. It is also used to carry the funerary caskets of retired firefighters. (Courtesy of the Lawrence E. Will Museum.)

The wonderful Herald Building, located at 427 Main Street in Belle Glade, has a stepped Zig-Zag roofline. Six tropical flamingos are divided in half by the central vertical lettering "Herald" in relief. The *Belle Glade Herald, c.* 1940, joined with the *Everglade Observer* to become the *Herald Observer* in 1979. In turn, it became the *Belle Glade Sun*, whose name was then shortened to the current moniker, the *Sun*.

The Old Frigidaire Building, a Maytag sales and repair facility and bridal gift shop, sits along Lake Okeechobee at 2015 East Main Street. Skeeter Boe's family, original pioneers who arrived in the early 1900s, still own the 1931 Art Moderne structure. Union carpenters worked for 50¢ an hour building the shop. The family plot remains on the property, and vintage signs still hang inside.

Rashley's Dry Cleaners was built in the 1940s alongside the historic Prince Theatre, at 331 East Main Street in Pahokee. For the last 10 years, Linda Joseph has been the executive director of Bright Ideas 2, a children's day care center, located in this classic symmetrical structure.

The Pahokee City Hall is located at 171 North Lake Avenue and was built by architect William Manly King. The adjoining Pahokee Fire Station and Pahokee Chamber of Commerce create a downtown city complex along the shore of Lake Okeechobee. Across the street is the famous Mister Jellyroll's coffee shop and gift boutique at 129 North Lake Avenue. (Courtesy of Ann O'Connell Rust.)

In the late 1920s, William Manly King built Canal Point Elementary School on Lake Okeechobee in the town of Canal Point. The institution taught grades one through eight and was built as an agricultural school, with an attached garden nursery. The historic structure, closed in 1988, now stands abandoned and destined for the wrecking ball because of neglect. Simon and Watkins, the first developers of the area, deeded the school property as land dedicated for "educational" purposes only. In the 1990s, community activists Dale Erickson, Roswell Harrington, and Vicki E. Silver led unsuccessful efforts in appealing to the Palm Beach County School District to renovate. A new school was built to the east of the property and opened as the Kathryn E. Cunningham/Canal Point Elementary School.

William Manly King built additions to Canal Point Elementary School in 1934. The Art Moderne building has vertical stepped-back columns and a stepped-down pyramid profile. Twin eagles are in mirrored image holding the flagpole. A papyrus leaf motif also surrounds the Federal-influenced Art Deco building. William Manly King (1886–1962) was born in Macon, Mississippi. He studied architecture and engineering at the Georgia School of Technology. William and his wife moved to South Florida in 1921. He was the Palm Beach School Board's architect through the 1920s and 1930s, building 90 percent of the public schools erected at that time. King was active in civic affairs and designed the city seal for West Palm Beach.

A marine architect designed the New Professional Building, completed in 1942, as a ship with porthole windows and a double pontoon (a floating structure used as a dock). Dr. H. (Harry) Hazedale Hipson Sr. arrived in Stuart in 1923 when the downtown only had electricity on Wednesday afternoons. Hipson left and went to practice dentistry in Jacksonville until 1924, when realtor John Taylor sent him a telegram announcing, "electricity all day, every day, come on down."

The building withstood the damage of the 1949 hurricane, and the dentist continued to practice in the Art Deco building until he passed away in 1969. Dr. Harry Hazedale "Dale" Hipson Jr. also practiced dentistry in the ship-like structure at 31–33 East Osceola Street. He retired in 1992 with his wife, Sue, and sold the building to Harlee Professional Service Medical Offices.

L. Phillips Clarke of West Palm Beach designed the Citizens Bank of Stuart at 256 Osceola Street in 1938. Years later, the bank received its national charter and became the First National Bank of Stuart. It was then the Professional Exchange Building and in the 1960s housed Florida Power and Light. The structure was remodeled into the Jolly Sailor, an English-style pub, and is currently Duffy's Sports Bar.

The Dehon Building is located at 11 East Osceola Street and is owned by the Arthur Dehon family. The curvilinear building is in the heart of historic downtown Stuart and is filled with boutiques, art galleries, and restaurants. The City of Stuart is dedicated to revitalizing its sense of community through preservation of distinctive historic architecture.

100

Seven

DECADENT DETAILS (COUNTYWIDE)

In the early years of Art Deco, architectural ornamentation drew upon stylized or simplified natural motifs such as the sun, water, and tropical flora and fauna. As time went by, design became more abstract, industrial, and geometric. The practitioners of the style became enamored with the sleek streamlined shapes derived from the principles of aerodynamics and the concept of "form following function."

The "decadent details" revealed in this chapter are scattered throughout Palm Beach County. Some photographs are components of buildings previewed in earlier chapters, while others display highlights seen for the first time. New materials were now available in the era of Modernism. Concrete, glass, iron, wood, chrome, and canvas are just a few that are reproduced on the following pages. Architects and designers used new and advanced technologies that allowed them to break away from outdated and traditional design.

Art Deco design is popular today because contemporary society can relate to and understand the progressive attitudes of the Machine Age. Daily life in the third millennium depends on "state of the art" inventions such as the cell phone, the Internet, lasers, and microwaves. Speed and streamlined technology, which were main themes of Modernism, are completely relevant for today's "life in the fast lane."

The wrought-iron gate at 2631 Flagler Drive, West Palm Beach, is the original entryway for the Wagner House. The symmetrical design is divided into three sections. There are three horizontal waves above and below the initial "W." Current owners Cheryl and Homer Marshman did a sensitive renovation and addition in 1999. Cleverly, the gate was inverted. The "W" was transformed into their initial, the letter "M." Artisans fabricated another matching iron gate to be displayed horizontally. It hangs as part of the electric driveway gate for the property on the corner of Flagler Drive and Belmonte Road, southeast of Belvedere Road.

Architect Maurice Fatio designed Villa Today, the Palm Beach mansion at 260 Via Bellaria for Mr. and Mrs. Charles Herrington Chadwick in 1932. The gateway doors are geometrically incised with a Greek Key design. Stylized African sculptures playing musical instruments sit atop fluted columns. (Courtesy of Preservation Foundation of Palm Beach.)

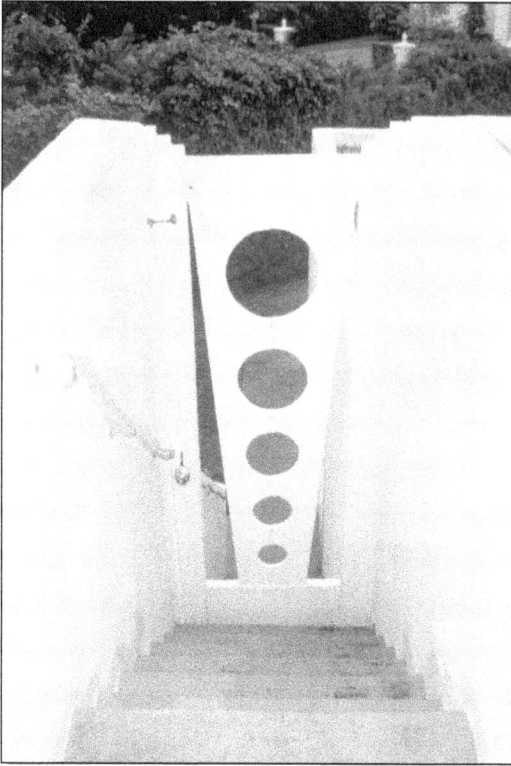

This Nautical Deco mansion fittingly named Fore and Aft, at 1221 North Lake Way, has a side staircase to an upper level. Five circular rings are cut out of a V-shaped gate that divides the stairwell. The repeated design symbolizes the highly revered V8-engine technology of the day. The stair railings are made of marine rope, and the concrete ledge has a Zig-Zag design. (Courtesy of Kirby Kooluris.)

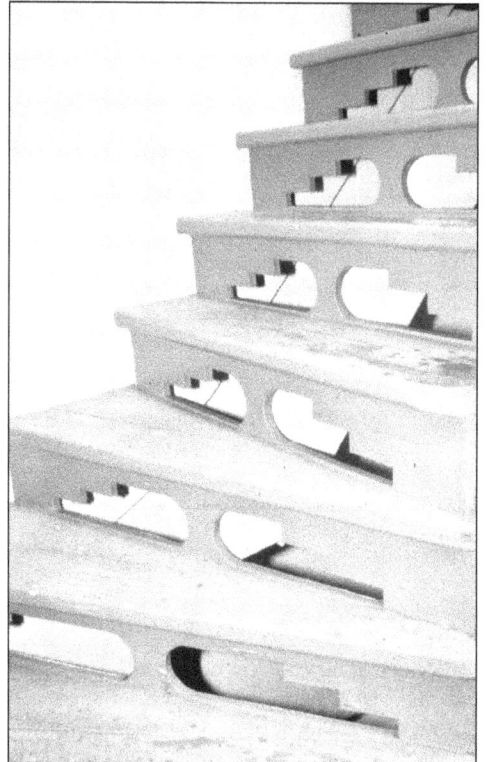

This photograph details the Belford Shoumate house built in 1937, shown above and in chapter five. The curved staircase of the Fore and Aft lands at an exterior gazebo-like portico on a private third-level deck. Each wooden riser has a double lightning bolt cutout with rounded corners reminiscent of a sleigh. (Courtesy of Kirby Kooluris.)

A private residence in Delray Beach, at 503 Northeast Second Avenue, is adorned with a Tropical Deco wrought-iron gate. The corner sun is cropped and has linear rays. A bending flamingo stands amid cattails, which are native to the South Florida Everglades. The photograph shows a second identical gate beyond the first gate.

This image from the Fore and Aft House in Palm Beach enlarges the V8-engine motif and is a salute to the Machine Age. The "8" is represented by two cutout circles, with the larger one on top. The design is encompassed by a third circular porthole, as shown in the south entrance of the nautical home's privacy wall. (Courtesy of Kirby Kooluris.)

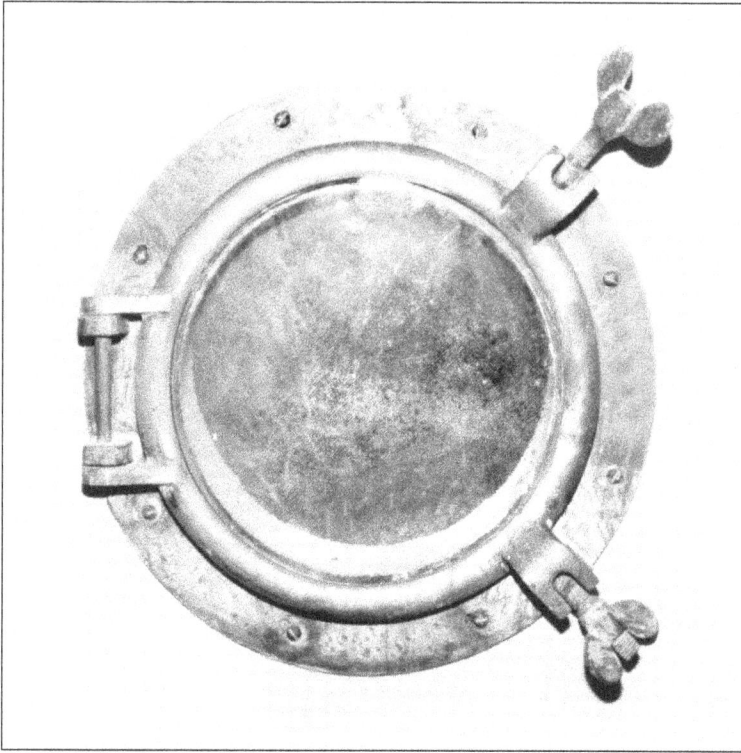

The Shopp House at 3135 Washington Road in West Palm Beach has an authentic porthole in an interior closet of the home. To create airflow and ventilation, the ship-like window is complete with metal frame, hinges, and locking bolts, and it opens to let fresh air circulate throughout the structure.

The stucco pyramid is the hallmark for the recent addition to the Wagner House, at 2631 Flagler Drive in West Palm Beach. Lake Worth landscape architect David Keir designed and supervised the construction of the three-dimensional swirls placed in the surrounding landscape. The Decometric swirl (original art created in the late 20th century to reflect the Art Deco style) sits in the poolside courtyard. (Courtesy of Cheryl and Homer Marshman.)

The Wagner House living room has a split-level entrance with a terrazzo floor. Three levels are created by the circular steps that look like concentric waves on a shoreline. The top and bottom landings are shades of tan while the middle step is a contrasting shade of green. (Courtesy of Cheryl and Homer Marshman.)

Shoumate's Fore and Aft House, at 1221 North Lake Way in Palm Beach, has a "ship ahoy" fireplace. The original fireplace ensemble includes twin freestanding anchors and a matching andiron rack. Fireplaces serve as both decorative and functional elements in structures without central heating. The adjoining wall on the right has three built-in "boat" shelves. (Courtesy of Kirby Kooluris.)

The U.S. Post Office in Palm Beach located at 95 North County Road is known as the Main Post Office. Mural artist Charles Rosen painted three panels in the lobby depicting life in early Florida. The panel that hangs on the left depicts the Intracoastal Waterway, the west side of the island. The center panel, not shown, depicts a historic Seminole Indian scene.

The First National Bank of Delray was built in 1929. Aaron T. Smock, a professional artist who specialized in painting flora and fauna, created this mural in 1956. He had a studio that overlooked Old School Square on Swinton Avenue. The original painting, featuring birds of the Everglades including herons, flamingos, and spoonbills, is now housed at the Delray Beach Historical Society. (Courtesy of the Delray Beach Historical Society.)

The Main Post Office lobby houses a triptych mural. The panel that hangs on the right depicts the Atlantic Ocean. In 1937, architect Louis A. Simon built the U.S. Post Office in the Mediterranean Revival style featuring exposed cypress beams in the lobby. On July 21, 1983, the structure was added to the U.S. National Register of Historic Places.

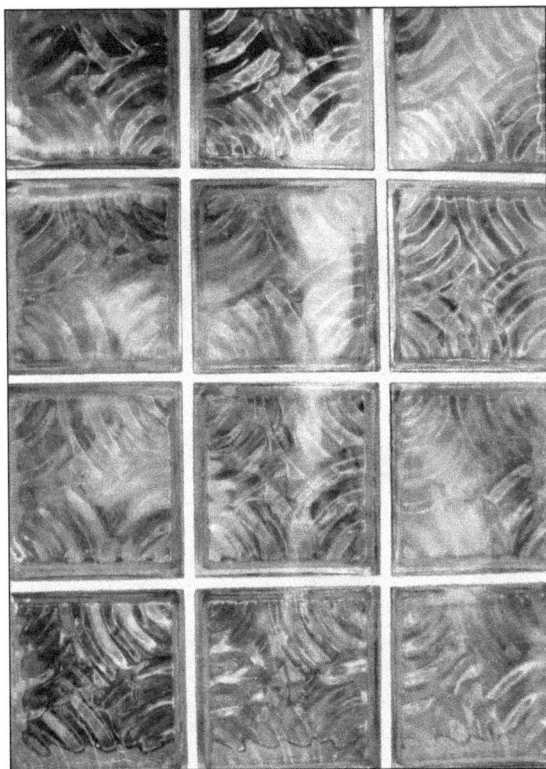

Glass block windows from the Victor and Eleanor Barbour House at 140 Monroe Drive in West Palm Beach are shown as an abstraction. Belford Shoumate's nautical theme is illustrated symbolically in glass. Drops of rainwater appear as ripples on a pond in the back courtyard of the fabulous home. Glass block diffusion is one of the most commonly used elements of Art Deco design. (Courtesy of Jean and Sumner Draper.)

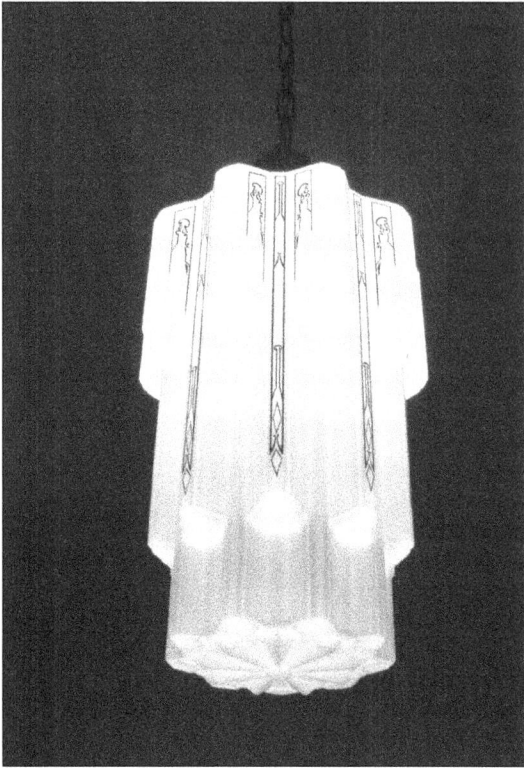

In 1934, G. Sherman Childs built the historic Lake Worth City Hall, 7 North Dixie Highway, as a Municipal Auditorium for the Work Progress Administration. Childs designed the white glass ceiling fixtures for the building's interior. Thin black lines are individually hand-painted on the hanging globes. The Museum of the City of Lake Worth displays 11 lights from the original auditorium. (Courtesy Museum of the City of Lake Worth.)

The triangular light fixture hangs on the exterior facade of the Wagner House in West Palm Beach. Cheryl and Homer Marshman had 11 Lalique-inspired lights custom made to illuminate the Art Deco mansion on the Intracoastal Waterway in West Palm Beach. Rene Jules Lalique (1860–1945) was a distinguished artist whose glasswork was a major influence during the Art Nouveau and Art Deco periods. (Courtesy of Cheryl and Homer Marshman.)

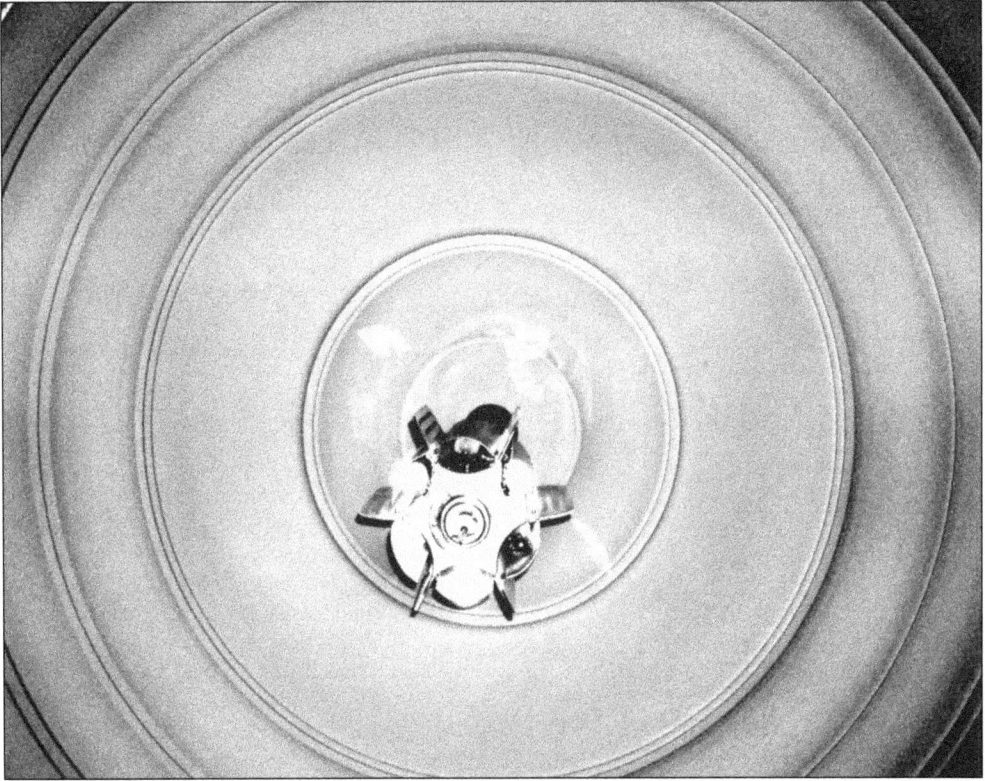

Centered over the grand staircase and seen from the front door is the sculptural second-floor ceiling of the Wagner House. Twirling concentric circles resemble the rings of the solar system. The stylized lighting fixture appears as if flames are emanating from a futuristic space capsule. (Courtesy of Cheryl and Homer Marshman.)

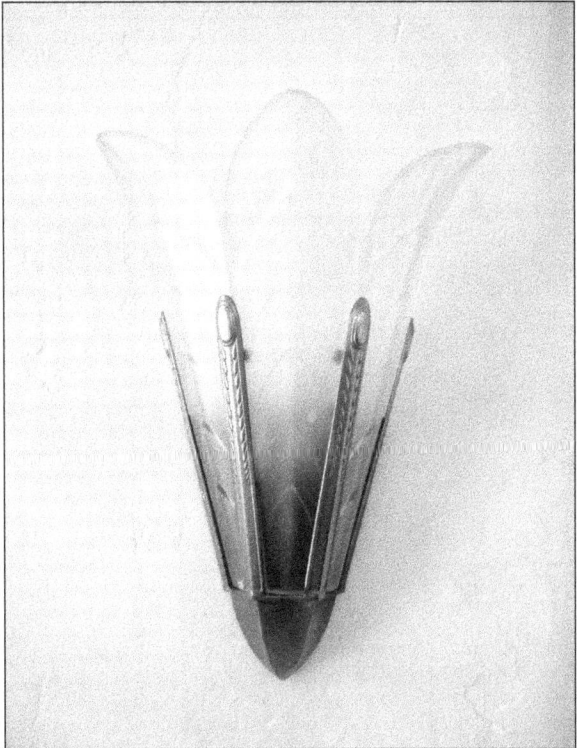

The tulip-shaped wall sconce hangs in the interior of the Wagner House in West Palm Beach. The tulip has three petals molded and etched with a linear design. In the Machine Age, it was popular to have glass etched, sandblasted, or enameled. The French lighting fixture originally hung in a 1930s hotel in Paris. (Courtesy of Cheryl and Homer Marshman.)

This stylized relief adorns the back courtyard wall of the Wagner House on Flagler Drive. Three swirls form an abstract floral design. Renowned West Palm Beach sculptor Rueben Hale created the relief for the Marshman family. Hale is a former chairperson of the Humanities Division of Palm Beach Community College. (Courtesy of Cheryl and Homer Marshman.)

The F. W. Woolworth Company Building is located at 314–316 Clematis Street in downtown West Palm Beach. Woolworth's was one of the original American five-and-dime stores popular in the Depression days. It was built in 1923 by contractor Franklin G. Mason and was then modified in 1932. The stylized floral bas-reliefs are set in from stepped vertical columns. The building is now the home of Z Gallerie, a national home-furnishing showroom.

This tropical open-relief is one of two stucco images located at 3016 South Olive Avenue. It is the only modern architectural element found on the Spanish Revival private residence in West Palm Beach. The cropped sun has linear rays, and the palm tree is in motion. The vertical swirling waves symbolize flowing water, a repeating Art Deco motif, also seen in the Wagner House below.

This is an original relief designed by Belford Shoumate at the Wagner House in West Palm Beach. The concrete ornamentation is a symmetrically balanced floral. The wave-like swirls continue the motif of the design that proudly spans the front entrance of the home on Flagler Drive. (Courtesy of Cheryl and Homer Marshman.)

This is a fabulous vintage hydraulic barbershop chair, made by the Emil J. Paidar Company of Chicago, Illinois. The classic red-and-white chair has an original signature and date of 1956. The streamlined chair has a curved barrel back and a circular chrome "button" and base. Emil J. Paidar has been making barbershop chairs and rotating barbershop signs since the start of the Twentieth Century. The Modern chair sits at the Shear Kut I Barber Shop at 611 Lake Avenue in Lake Worth. The Art Moderne structure, built in the 1940s, has an eyebrow and fluted ribbed facade just a few doors away from the Lake Avenue Theatre. Vintage men's grooming and shaving paraphernalia fill the storefront window of the shop. The owner and operator of the barbershop, Franklin L. Reed, has been cutting men's hair for several decades.

Eight

ART DECO SOCIETY OF THE PALM BEACHES (POLITICS AND PARTIES)

Sharon Koskoff was a member of the Art Deco Society of New York in the early 1980s. She was known as the "Art Deco Lady" who painted "super-graphic" murals in the Decometric style. In 1985, Koskoff moved to Delray Beach, Florida. The following year, she met Barbara Baer Capitman, founder of the Miami Design Preservation League, who convinced her to organize the Art Deco Society of the Palm Beaches. The first organizational meeting was August 5, 1987. The historic preservation group incorporated on January 27, 1988, and became a not-for-profit 501(c)3 organization on January 14, 1994.

The original founding members were Alan Bernstein, David Bittner, Elaine Schneider, Gloria Fruchter, Ira Schneider, Kris Bauer, Loretta Smith, Mark Smith, Samuel Brams, and Sharon Koskoff. New enthusiasts Amy Clyman, Anne Weir, David Edgar, Donna Kay Blodgett, Soni Fine, and Sylvia Resnick came on board shortly after.

The mission of the Art Deco Society of the Palm Beaches is to promote education, preservation, and awareness of Art Deco and Twentieth Century art, architecture, and design. The society works to obtain listings of buildings for placement on the National Register of Historic Places. Hundreds of architectural treasures have been identified, and a network of Art Deco enthusiasts has been brought together.

The Art Deco Society of the Palm Beaches is a member of the Palm Beach County Cultural Council, the Florida Trust for Historic Preservation, the National Trust for Historic Preservation, and the International Coalition of Art Deco Societies. For current events, visit the Web site www.artdecoPB.org.

Private Party on Peruvian was held on February 23, 1991, at the Palm Beach home of Michele Wood and her husband, Jonathan Cameron-Hayes. Standing from left to right are Michael Kinerk and Dennis Wilhelm (coauthors of *Rediscovering Art Deco U.S.A.*), Sharon Koskoff (president of the Art Deco Society of the Palm Beaches), and Kirby Kooluris (owner of Fore and Aft).

Dozens of Deco enthusiasts attended the Second Annual Show and Tell at the Addison, Boca Raton, in winter 1991. Presenters are, from left to right, (first row) Mark Smith (vice president) and Jackie Alperin; (second row) Sharon Koskoff, Sylvia Resnick, Gloria Fruchter (secretary), Anne Weir (artist representative), and Loretta Smith (special events). From spaceships to salad servers, an extraordinary variety of treasured Art Deco antiques adorned the Grand Salon.

Barbara Baer Capitman, the "Queen of Art Deco" (left), sits with Sharon Koskoff while at the Miami Beach home of French antique dealer Nicole Sultan. Earlier that morning, January 16, 1988, Capitman presented Koskoff with an Appreciation Award signed by Stephen P. Clark, mayor of Metropolitan Dade County, Florida. Barbara was Sharon's mentor and guided her through the process of starting an Art Deco society. Barbara Baer Capitman initiated the birth of many Art Deco societies across America, changing people's lives as she touched them with her magic wand. She taught Sharon about preservation, identification of architectural styles, organizational skills, and the rewards of a media press release. In 1976, Barbara started the Miami Design Preservation League, and by 1979, "Old Miami Beach" was listed on the National Register of Historic Places. Koskoff and Capitman remained best of friends until March 30, 1990, when Barbara died at age 69. She will always be remembered for keeping the "Art" in Art Deco, as her magnificent legacy lives on.

In November 1989, Wallace Harper and Linda Fleetwood share conversation at the Fore and Aft House by Belford Shoumate. The two familiar faces of the art world attended the second Art Deco private residence party in the Palm Beach home of Kirby Kooluris. The futuristic home was the host to several other membership parties for Art Deco Society of the Palm Beaches patrons.

Members enjoy a glass of Art Deco Wines of Style by Alexis Lichine in 1988. From left to right are Diane Alperin, David Bittner, and Jay Alperin, D.D.S. Bittner, a journalist, was on the founding Art Deco Society of the Palm Beaches board of directors. He moved to Ohio in the year 2000. Jay Alperin became the mayor of Delray Beach from 1996 to 2000 and continues his strong support of Art Deco activities.

On November 25, 1990, Canal Street Grille had an opening celebration for Decometric murals, wooden cutouts, and etched glass by artist Sharon Koskoff. Cheering on is member Cheryl Kerner (left) and Jill Grossman, vacationing from New York. Formerly the Bridge Restaurant, the grille was located in the Streamline Moderne Boyd Building. After extensive renovation by Busch's Restaurant, Koskoff's murals are gone, but the large etched-glass storefront windows remain.

Dressed for the nautically themed party in 1988 at the Fore and Aft House are Rubin (left) and Shirley Koskoff, the parents of Sharon Koskoff. "Poppa Ruby" works with his daughter on mural and design projects. The Koskoffs volunteer their organizational skills at preservation events. Behind the pair hangs one of the Nathan Dolinsky paintings of the four seasons in the Palm Beach house at 1221 North Lake Way.

At Matinee in May, on Sunday, May 20, 1990, Elaine (left) and Ira Schneider (former vice president of the Art Deco Society) take part in the social gathering at Antique Emporium in Pompano Beach of Broward County. They were instrumental in establishing the Art Deco Society of the Palm Beaches. Elaine is a visual artist who created Art Deco fashion illustrations, and Ira owned a sculptural glass studio in Lake Worth.

Sumner (left) and Jean Draper have been loyal patrons of the Art Deco Society of the Palm Beaches since its inception in 1987. They have opened their home at 140 Monroe Drive in West Palm Beach to many visitors. They have hosted both private membership parties and motorcoach tours, allowing hundreds of preservationists to view the historic Nautical Deco residence built by Belford Shoumate in 1933.

The Victor and Eleanor Barbour House, owned by Jean and Sumner Draper, hosted a viewing for the National Society of Colonial Dames of America on January 12, 1994. Standing is Sharon Koskoff (left) with Mary E. "Liz" Perial in the rear patio of the ship-like home. Liz is an Art Deco advocate, arts patron, and a longtime docent at the Norton Museum of Art in West Palm Beach.

Put on your sunscreen for Deco in Delray walking tours, on East Atlantic Avenue, in downtown Delray Beach. This tour photograph was taken on December 10, 2004. On the far left are Jay and Diane Alperin (holding the itinerary) with their friend Nicholas Ritchie (in between them) with hat and sunglasses. Others remain unidentified. The tour begins at Boston's on the Beach and ends at the Sundy House for lunch.

On August 19 and 20, 1989, Stoltz Brothers generously provided the Arbern Financial Centre, 301 Yamato Road in Boca Raton, for Deco Days '89. Its glass curtain walls, indoor fountains, soaring atrium skylight, and unique floor plan of distinctive Zig-Zag angles provided breathtaking surroundings. Deco Days '89 had 36 exhibiting artists and antique vendors, an antique car show, and dozens of sponsors including WXEL, IBM, and Southeast Bank.

Deco Days '89 was a Boca Festival Days event, created to attract art and cultural programming in the quiet summer months. Costumed in official festival T-shirt and green sequined bow-ties are, from left to right, Soni Fine, Sharon Koskoff, and Sam Brams. Soni is a contributing member of the Art Deco Society of the Palm Beaches. Sam is one of the original founding board members who helped establish the organization.

On November 19, 2004, the Deco in Delray walking tour concluded with lunch at the historic Sundy House. Built in 1902 as a feed house, it is listed on the National Register of Historic Places. The Sundy House features a restaurant, 11 luxurious guest rooms, the Roux Bamboux Lounge, and the tropical scenery of Taru Gardens. It claims to be Florida's only hotel with a freshwater swimming pond.

Linda Fleetwood of the Delray Beach Community Redevelopment Association commissioned Sharon Koskoff to create a poster for a new event entitled Art and Jazz on the Avenue. Koskoff's highly collectible poster was used during the first two years. The Art Deco Society of the Palm Beaches presented a lecture by Boca Raton architect Winslow Elliott Wedin on March 19, 1991, at the bimonthly festival observed on Thursday nights.

ART & JAZZ on the AVENUE

Atlantic Avenue
Delray Beach

Thursday, March 19th
5 pm - 12 midnight

Art Deco Society of the
Palm Beaches
Lecture by Winslow Elliott
Wedin "Modern Urban
Architecture" 7:30pm
Photographic exhibit of Deco
buildings in Palm Beach
County 5-11pm

South Beach Blast is an annual one-day bus trip to Miami Beach. On January 17, 1999, Carolyn Zimmerman (left) and Jeanne Kurth, both of Delray Beach, enjoy lunch at the Governor's Hotel, 435 Twenty-first Street. Carolyn is a community activist, and Jeanne is a volunteer at Old School Square. The tour group attended the Art Deco Weekend street festival on Ocean Drive filled with art, antiques, jazz, and nostalgia.

Artwheels, an educational outreach program of the Art Deco Society of the Palm Beaches, provides art and architectural tours. On March 15, 2001, members of Artisans Unlimited from Martin County visit the Renaissance Fair at Vizcaya Museum and Gardens in Miami. Artisans board the luxury motorcoach, breakfasting on "mimosas and muffins" enroute to the Historic Biltmore Hotel in Coral Gables.

At a more recent South Beach Blast bus trip on March 21, 2004, members dine at the five-star Mark's South Beach, in the Nash Hotel at 1120 Collins Avenue in Miami Beach. Seated on the left is R. David Goldsticker, with his cousins Lee and Helene Goldsticker. Seated to the right is Port St. Lucie visual artist Arlene Canty.

Participants listen intently to an educational lecture entitled "Art Deco Dress and Fashion" by guest speaker Susannah Worth, Ph.D., a costume and textiles historian. On January 3, 2002, the event was a component of Art Deco First Thursdays, a three-part lecture series. At the Armory Art Center in West Palm Beach are Sharon Koskoff (left) and Jennifer Ward (center). The remainder of the group is unidentified.

On April 2, 2006, approximately 30 members of the Art Deco Society of the Palm Beaches attended a Show and Tell at the Wenger House in Delray Beach. Owner Linda Stabile showed her home while other presenters shared their art, antiques, and vintage memorabilia. Standing from left to right are Sharri Roser, Richard Roser, Amy Clyman, Linda Stabile, Calvin Zimmer, and David Larsen, who all joined in the festivities.

Dr. Robert A. Flucke (left) and his wife, Mary, drove their 1940 Lincoln Zephyr Continental Cabriolet to the Show and Tell in Delray Beach. In 1956, the Fluckes purchased the Bennington Gray automobile, becoming the automobile's third owners. The vintage Ford won Best in Show at the 2002 Lincoln Continental National Meet. Robert and Mary are "snowbirds" from Three Rivers, Michigan, and spend their winters in North Palm Beach.

On Sunday, April 23, 1989, artist Sharon Koskoff peers over the roof of the freshly painted Robert and Mary Montgomery Armory Art Center. She led a volunteer effort to paint the building in stylish Decometric colors of peach, mint and lavender. The composition of the new palette revealed the hidden architectural elements of the Art Deco treasure. Koskoff was an instructor at the art center from 1988 until 2003.

Demolition is forever! On a cloudy December 19, 2005, the bulldozer destroyed a Nautical Art Deco building at 1038 East Atlantic Avenue and Gleason Street in Delray Beach. Along with it went an entire city block, leveled to the ground in the name of progress. Preservation, education, and awareness of Twentieth Century design and Modernism must prevail in order for future generations to move forward into the "World of Tomorrow."

Visit us at
arcadiapublishing.com

www.ingramcontent.com/pod-product-compliance
Lightning Source LLC
Chambersburg PA
CBHW080553110426
42813CB00006B/1299